STUDYING FOR HISTORY

STUDYING FOR HISTORY

DAVID PACE
Indiana University

SHARON L. PUGH
Indiana University

BRENDA D. SMITH, Series Editor
Georgia State University

HarperCollins*CollegePublishers*

Acquisitions Editor: Ellen Schatz
Project Coordination, Text and Cover Design: Ruttle Graphics, Inc.
Electronic Production Manager: Angel Gonzalez Jr.
Manufacturing Manager: Willie Lane
Electronic Page Makeup: Ruttle Graphics, Inc.
Printer and Binder: R. R. Donnelley & Sons Company
Cover Printer: The Lehigh Press, Inc.

Studying for History

Library of Congress Cataloging-in-Publication Data

Pace, David, 1944–
    Studying for history/David Pace, Sharon L. Pugh.
        p.   cm.
    Includes index.
    ISBN 0-06-500649-6
    1. History—Study and teaching (Higher)—United States.   I. Pugh, Sharon L.   II. Title.
    D16.3.P33   1995   95-12331
    907.1'173—dc20   CIP

95 96 97 98 9 8 7 6 5 4 3 2 1

To Kate Hess Pace and B. K. Sharma

CONTENTS

ACKNOWLEDGMENTS   ix

CHAPTER 1 GETTING STARTED:
           THE BIG PICTURE   1

ORIENTING YOURSELF IN A NEW PLACE   2
GETTING YOUR BEARINGS IN YOUR HISTORY COURSE   3
CREATING YOUR OWN MAPS   5
SCOUTING A WORLD HISTORY COURSE   8

CHAPTER 2 DIFFERENT KINDS OF HISTORY   13

THE NATURE OF HISTORY TODAY   14
POLITICS, WAR, AND DIPLOMACY   17
INTELLECTUAL AND CULTURAL HISTORY   19
SOCIAL HISTORY   25
WOMEN AND GENDER STUDIES   28
THE ABUNDANCE OF HISTORY   30

CHAPTER 3 MANAGING YOUR
           ENERGY, TIME, AND MIND   35

MOTIVATION: FINDING YOUR OWN ENERGY   36
TIME MANAGEMENT   44

CHAPTER 4 THINKING LIKE A HISTORIAN   59

THE HISTORIAN AS DETECTIVE   60
THE HISTORIAN AS JUDGE   67
THE HISTORIAN AS LAWYER   72

CHAPTER 5   READING STRATEGIES FOR LEARNING HISTORY   85

STRATEGIC READING   86
ANALYTICAL READING   87
NOTE-CARD TECHNIQUES   96
MAKING MAPS   99
PRIMARY SOURCES   106
WHEN TO READ? BEFORE OR AFTER THE LECTURE?   108

CHAPTER 6   STUDY STRATEGIES FOR LEARNING HISTORY   113

LEARNING FROM LECTURES   114
GETTING THE MOST OUT OF DISCUSSION   124

CHAPTER 7   PREPARING FOR AND TAKING EXAMS   139

PREPARATION STRATEGIES   140
PERFORMANCE STRATEGIES: TAKING THE TEST   145
EXAM QUESTIONS   148
ESSAY QUESTIONS   155
OTHER TYPES OF EXAMS   166

CHAPTER 8   WRITING PAPERS   171

BASIC COMPONENTS OF A HISTORY PAPER   172
BUILDING A PAPER   176
GIVING CREDIT WHERE CREDIT'S DUE   186
CONDUCTING RESEARCH   190

GLOSSARY   197

INDEX   207

ACKNOWLEDGMENTS

We want to thank the following people for their invaluable consultation and assistance in the preparation of this manuscript: Elizabeth Agnew, Casey Blake, Roni Goveia, Esther and Buddy Gray, James Madison, Lisa Maidi, Mary Porter, Tom Prasch, Todd Weinman.

ACKNOWLEDGMENTS

CHAPTER 1

GETTING STARTED: THE BIG PICTURE

GETTING FOCUSED

- *How can you use this book to help you succeed in history courses?*

- *How can you use the syllabus and the table of contents and chapter summaries in your textbook to get the big picture of a course before it even begins?*

- *How can you find out what topics, geographical information, and dates are important in this course?*

ORIENTING YOURSELF IN A NEW PLACE

Imagine you were a new European colonist living in the early 1600s, shipwrecked and alone on your first trip to North America. Your prospects would be rather bleak. There would be potential sources of food and shelter around you, but you would not know how to take advantage of them. There would be landmarks that theoretically could help you find the way to settlements, but they would be of little use without some prior knowledge of the territory. It would be a matter of chance if you ever found your way to civilization or discovered a means of staying alive in the wilderness.

By contrast, a Native American or an experienced European woodsman might thrive in the same wilderness. For this individual, the forest would provide all that was needed for success. The mountains, rivers, and stars would all be part of a mental map that would provide instant orientation. This inhabitant of the wilderness might even derive excitement and a sense of self-worth in the same territory that threatened to destroy the newcomer.

The only difference between the shipwreck survivor and the experienced woodsman is knowledge—practical knowledge concerning how to operate in a particular setting. The inexperienced person does not know how to use the environment. He or she feels lost. The surroundings seem disorienting or even hostile. The person with knowledge, by contrast, feels at home and can make use of all that the forest has to offer.

Many students experience history courses as if they had been shipwrecked in the wilderness. They feel they are lost in a vast continent of dates, events, and concepts. They have no idea how to chart a path across the new territory or how to make use of the resources around them. When their first efforts to deal with their surroundings fail, they give up or hope that some miraculous insight will save them.

Yet, all it takes to transform a history course from a hostile wilderness into a familiar and supporting environment is a little practical knowledge. It is that knowledge that this book intends to provide. Think of this book as a "field guide," designed to help you orient yourself in your history course. It will suggest which paths lead to success in history. It will provide practical hints, so that you can turn lectures, readings, and discussions into useful tools for achieving your goals. It will further your understanding of how history operates today, and, hopefully, it will help you to share in the excitement that most historians feel for their subject.

This book will be useful, however, only if you take charge of your own education. The best field guide in the world would be of no use to the explorer who just sat under a tree or who was distracted by every passing butterfly. You must make active use of this book. You will have to try the exercises contained in it and apply its lessons to your own course. Only then will it open up new possibilities of mastery for you. If you use this book wisely, it will make you a pioneer, successfully taming a new land.

GETTING YOUR BEARINGS IN YOUR HISTORY COURSE

"You Gotta Know the Territory"

As we have indicated, it is crucial for your success that you find your bearings as soon as possible. Fortunately, you don't have to be a Daniel Boone to become oriented in a history class. Others have gone through this land before, and they have left maps and signposts that can help guide you along your way.

Using these guides, you can begin to get the big picture of the course even before you begin systematic exploration. You can get an idea of what is most important to your instructor and what you should emphasize when you are reading, taking notes, participating in discussion, or preparing for exams. You also can begin to develop a strategy for success and a rough schedule of the more demanding and less demanding periods of the course.

Seeing the big picture will be easier if you begin to draw your mental maps as soon as you get the textbook or read the syllabus. This will save you a lot of time and help you understand what is going on right from the start.

Finding Maps

The best place to begin generally is the **syllabus**. Syllabi differ widely, but most will give you some kind of overview of the issues that you will encounter in the course. Look at the topics covered, the time periods into which the course is divided, and the terminology used. All of these can serve to help you understand what will be important in the course. In addition, the schedule of assignments and exams can help you create a plan for managing your time throughout the semester.

Your textbook's table of contents can also provide invaluable assistance in preparing your initial map. What are the major sections of the textbook? What are the major issues or themes covered in the reading? In many textbooks, there are special summaries or study questions at the beginning and/or end of each chapter or section. Reading through all of these at the start of the semester can provide you with an invaluable overview of the territory ahead. In addition, the glossary of your textbook provides an often overlooked resource. Use it to look up and find definitions or explanations of unfamiliar terms in the syllabus, table of contents, and summaries. Finally, your textbook's index indicates to you how much coverage is given to the ideas, people, events, and topics contained in the textbook. (You might begin by examining the index located at the end of this book to get an idea of what sorts of things we will be covering.)

INITIAL GUIDEPOSTS IN A HISTORY COURSE

- the syllabus
- the textbook's table of contents
- summaries at the beginning or end of chapters
- the glossary
- the index
- other books that summarize the course material

If the syllabus, the table of contents, and the other textbook features we mentioned do not seem to offer clear guideposts, or if you want to gain an even clearer overview, you might search for a book that summarizes the material you will be studying. Keep in mind, however, that you must be prepared at every moment of the course to replace this initial, somewhat crude map with more sophisticated images of the territory. Nonetheless, it can often provide a bird's-eye view of the entire period, which will help you keep your bearings as the semester progresses.

■

PERSONAL LEARNING QUESTIONS

**Why is it desirable to get the big picture before
you begin work in a history course?
Where can you look to get the big picture of the
course at the beginning of the semester?**

■

CREATING YOUR OWN MAPS

Finding the General Issues

As you develop your initial map, you will need to get an idea of the
topics or types of issues and problems that will be addressed in the
course. This is usually not difficult to do. Even a superficial glance at
the materials for a survey of U.S. history since 1865, for example, might
indicate that the first part of the course is going to focus on such topics
as the reconstruction of the nation after the Civil War, the economic expansion of the late nineteenth century, and the desire to reform the
new industrial America.

Each of these topics can serve as a category in a kind of mental filing cabinet. As you take in information and concepts, you can file them
away immediately in the appropriate "folders." By so doing, you will
be able to see what is most important in the lectures and the readings.
And, when you begin to study for exams, you will find you have already made great strides toward organizing the information.

Understanding the Geography of History

When you begin to draw a geographical map, you need to know what
are the major divisions of the territory. Is the land divided into various
political units? Are there areas of mountains and areas of plains?

Similar questions arise in history. Historical information is almost
always organized geographically. If your instructor is lecturing on the
impact of the cultures of Mesopotamia on that of ancient Greece, you
will need to have some idea where the two regions were.

Therefore, a few minutes spent studying the maps in the textbook
or in a historical atlas can make the entire course easier to understand.
It is rarely necessary to memorize every detail of the maps, but you

should be able to identify the major divisions on a blank map and have an idea of how these major divisions changed over time.

Understanding Periods in History

History is organized in time as well as in space. Just as you will need to know the boundaries between two nations, you will need to know the boundaries between two time periods. Historians automatically divide the past into eras, each with certain prominent features. If your instructor is lecturing on the Ming dynasty in China, early modern Europe, or the **antebellum** United States, for example, you will need to have at least a rough idea of the years (or centuries) included in each period and the period's general character. These time units are usually obvious from the syllabus or the textbook's table of contents. However, if you are still confused about the basic divisions, most instructors or teaching assistants will be glad to help you get your bearings.

It is important to remember that the definitions of periods are rarely precise. No one believes that the Middle Ages began on a particular day at 3:31 P.M. Periods of transition always exist at the beginning and end of eras. Moreover, historians often disagree as to exactly when it becomes appropriate to use a term such as *medieval*.

Understanding the Usefulness of Dates

There is, perhaps, no area in which popular ideas of history differ more from those of professional historians than dates. For many people, memorizing dates is the essence of history. For historians, dates are just useful signposts for organizing the past.

Without dates, the past tends to run together. It is difficult to know when one period has ended and another has begun. If you do not know that the Civil War ended in 1865, for example, you will find it difficult to understand the difference between race relations in the 1850s and those in the 1870s. In addition, without dates, it is difficult to understand the relationship between two events. It may be important, for example, to understand that the Reign of Terror came before the rise of Napoleon, and it is difficult to keep that straight without knowing roughly the dates of each.

On the other hand, there are more potential dates in any period than you could possibly memorize. Therefore, the point is to find those dates that are most important and organize your learning around them. In a history course on early modern Europe, for example, you might want to memorize the following dates: 1789 (beginning of the French Revolution); 1815 (end of Napoleonic era); 1848 (outbreak of revolutions across Europe, frustration of liberal hopes); 1870–1871 (defeat of France, unification of Germany, rise of nationalism); 1914 (outbreak of World War I); 1917 (Bolshevik Revolution in Russia); 1933 (Hitler comes to power); and 1945 (end of World War II). These eight dates can serve to break up this century and a half and organize your studying.

It is important to adjust to the particular course you are taking. In another European history course, the choice of crucial dates might differ from our earlier example. Moreover, a course that emphasizes social or intellectual history might focus less on dates than a course that emphasizes politics and diplomacy. In most cases, however, at least a few dates are crucial for organizing your studying. Certain dates may stand
(continued page 8)

A CENTURY AHEAD, COUNTING BACKWARDS, AND A LITTLE LATIN

There are three aspects of historical dates that sometimes confuse students. The first involves counting centuries. The period between A.D. 1 and A.D. 99 is called the first century. The period between A.D. 100 and A.D. 199 is called the second century, and so on. As a result, a date in the 100s is in the second century, and so on. Thus you may read on one page of a textbook that the Protestant Reformation took place in the sixteenth century, and on the next page that Martin Luther began the Reformation in 1517. There is no contradiction here, for 1517 *was* in the sixteenth century. We are less surprised to hear that 1945 is in the twentieth century, but it is the same principle. (We count our ages the same way. We are one year old at the end of our first year of life, and we are eighteen years old in the nineteenth year of life.)

Second, our dating system begins at A.D. 0 and moves forward. However, for dates before 0, it is necessary to count backward. Thus, 300 B.C. is *before* 200 B.C. Julius Caesar was born in 100 B.C. and died in 44 B.C.

Finally, in reading history you will sometime find dates such as c1713. The "c" stands for the Latin word **circa,** which means "around" or "about." Historians use this abbreviation when they know approximately when something happened, but do not know the exact date. Therefore, *c1713* means "around 1713."

---

out in the readings and lectures. If not, you might ask your instructor what he or she thinks are the ten or twelve most important dates in the period you are studying.

CREATING YOUR OWN MAPS

1. What general issues will be covered in your history course between now and the next exam? Why is it useful to be able to answer this question?
2. What do you need to know about geography to do well in this course? Can you find on a map all of the basic geographical units mentioned in the lectures and readings?
3. Into what periods is your history course divided? What are the general characteristics of each period?
4. What are the most important dates that you have to know in your history course? Why is each one important?

SCOUTING A WORLD HISTORY COURSE

Survey the Textbook

Thus far we have been describing this initial scouting of the course in very general terms. Now, let us examine in detail a particular example of such an exploratory scouting expedition in the territory of a specific history course.

Imagine that you are taking the first half of a two-semester course on world history. You realize that you are going to be faced with material about many cultures and periods. How can you establish your bearings at the very beginning of the course?

One way to do this is to spend a few minutes looking over the textbook.[1] You can begin with the table of contents. The material that you will cover this semester is divided into three parts, and these parts are subdivided into 21 chapters:

---

[1] In this exercise, we will be using Richard L. Greaves, Robert Zaller, Philip V. Cannistraro, and Rhoads Murphey, *Civilizations of the World: The Human Adventure* (New York: Harper and Row, 1990).

Part One: The Peoples and Cultures of Antiquity

1. The Societies of Western Asia and Egypt

2. Ancient India

3. The Formation of China

4. Early and Classical Greece

5. The Greek Achievement and the Hellenistic World

6. The Romans

7. Ancient World Religions

Part Two: The Middle Ages

8. Byzantium and Islam

9. Africa and the Americas Before 1500

10. Medieval India and Southeast Asia

11. A Golden Age in East Asia

12. The Rise of Europe

13. Life and Culture in Medieval Europe

14. Crisis and Recovery in Europe

15. New Horizons: The European Renaissance

Part Three: The Early Modern World

16. The Reformation

17. The Age of European Discovery

18. State-Building and Revolution

19. Islamic Empires in the Early Modern World

20. Imperial Revival in China

21. The Societies of the Early Modern World

You have learned a good deal about the course already. You know that the material will be divided into three big periods: Antiquity, the Middle Ages, and the Early Modern World. You will need to learn the characteristics of each period, but that can wait until later.

You also know some of the important topics in the course. In the first section, for example, you will be studying the early societies of Egypt and Western Asia, the creation of Indian, Chinese, Greek, and Roman culture, and the development of world religions. You can thumb through this section, glancing at the maps scattered through the textbook to make sure you understand the basic geography assumed in the course.

If you examine Chapter 6 in the textbook, "The Romans," you can get a clear overview of what will be expected of you, just by turning pages. Skimming the first paragraph of the chapter will give you a good idea of why the Romans were important. Turning the page you will see a map of Italy and a section head that reads "The Etruscans." The next section, "Early Rome," has two subsections: "From Monarchy to Republic" and "The Republic: Conflict and Accommodation." The next section, entitled "The Unification of Italy and the Conquest of the Mediterranean," contains subsections on "The Punic Wars" and "Conquests in the East."

The chapter continues in a similar vein. Now, let us stop here and consider for a moment what you already know about the course. You can now tell yourself: "When we get to the Roman chapter in the section on Antiquity, we will study the rise to power of the Romans as they moved from a monarchy to a republic and conquered first the rest of Italy and then the entire Mediterranean." You know that you will have to learn who the Etruscans were and who fought the Punic Wars. That can wait, however.

You can examine the entire textbook in this fashion in about an hour. If there is a special section on the history of artwork, you can glance through it and get some visual images to go with what you will be hearing in the lectures. The maps will give you a general idea of the geography of the course. Main themes and time periods will emerge automatically.

At the end of the hour, you will have a general framework for the course. You can look back over the syllabus to see if the same topics are emphasized there. And, you might even want to seek out students who did well in the course in previous semesters. They can help you add more details to the course map that you have developed.

Be Ready to Face the Semester

Devoting an hour or two to such preparations at the beginning of a semester can make a vital difference in your experience of a class. A general overview of the main themes, time periods, and geographical subdivisions of the course can keep you from getting lost. This overview also can help you get back on track quickly if you do become confused. Now when you listen to the lectures or read the textbook, you will know how to file away your new knowledge in the appropriate section of your brain. And, you will begin to have criteria for deciding what is important and what is not important.

You will, of course, have to refine this map as you get to know the territory in ever greater detail. In addition, there may be times when you discover that entire sections of your map need to be discarded. However, if you begin the semester with this kind of framework, you will be in a good position to organize new ideas as they come in. This will give you a sense of control and understanding, which can make the difference between success and failure.

APPLICATION EXERCISES

1. Produce a one-page summary of the material that you are going to cover in your history course this semester. What are the three or four biggest issues you will cover?

2. Make a tentative list of what you think you will need to know in this course. Be sure to include terms from the syllabus and textbook headings, geographic information, and important periods. What large questions might you be expected to answer?

3. Find a student who received a good grade in this history course in a past semester. Ask him or her to read over your summary of the material and your list of what you will need to know. Get as much feedback from this person as you can.

TERMS TO KNOW

A.D.

antebellum

B.C.

circa

early modern Europe

syllabus

CHAPTER 2

DIFFERENT KINDS OF HISTORY

GETTING FOCUSED

- *Why is it important to learn to think like a historian?*
- *How has history changed in the past several decades?*
- *What kinds of issues are important in the history course you are taking?*
- *Why is it important to recognize the differences among political, military, diplomatic, intellectual and cultural, and social history?*
- *How can understanding the notion of social class help you to understand history?*
- *Why is it important to distinguish between the terms* sex *and* gender *when studying history?*

THE NATURE OF HISTORY TODAY

Your success as an undergraduate depends on your ability to adjust to your surroundings. When you are in a chemistry class, you will do best if you think like a chemist. To do well in English, you should learn to read books as a literary critic would. Therefore, to do well in a history course, you must learn to read like a historian, write like a historian, and, most important, think like a historian.

To think like a historian, you may have to leave behind certain notions about history. High school teachers and the general culture sometimes present an outdated picture of what **contemporary** historians actually do. In this section of the textbook, we will help bring you up-to-date. This chapter will focus on the ways in which history has changed in recent decades and how those changes can affect your course. This chapter also will look at some of the different kinds of history being taught today.

The purpose of this chapter is to help you understand what you can expect in typical college history courses. It is very important, however, to pay attention to the nature of the specific course you are taking. The subjects emphasized in your course may differ from those described in this chapter. Therefore, you can use the suggestions in this section as a general guide. Just make sure that you adjust to the demands of your own course.

■

Personal Learning Questions

Think about the history courses you took before you got to college. What were they like? Were the issues covered in those courses similar to the issues covered in your current history course?

■

Do You Know What History Is?

Most people think they know what history is. In the past few decades, however, historians have changed their approaches to understanding the past. These changes constitute a major shift in the field of history. Therefore, the notions you bring to the study of history may need to be revised.

Let us see how up-to-date you are. Take the following quiz before continuing to read this chapter.

WHAT IS HISTORY?
A POP QUIZ

Indicate whether the following statements are true or false.

1. Unlike the sciences, the subject matter of history has remained more or less the same over the past century. _____
2. Students of history must be able to readily memorize facts. _____
3. History is the story of the actions of famous men. _____
4. History deals primarily with public events and leaves culture to departments of literature and art history. _____
5. History deals with aspects of human life, such as politics, that change, not with the eternal givens of human existence such as birth, sex, and death. _____
6. Only people who could leave written records are the subjects of history. _____

Most professional historians would have answered false to all of these questions. They do not view history primarily as a set of facts to be memorized. They do not believe that the study of the past should be limited to recounting the deeds of famous men. They study the literature and **culture** of the past, as well as everything from architecture to advertising. They deal with the ways that birth, life, death, sex, and being male or female have been explained and experienced through the ages. And, they study the masses of society, as well as personal biographies.

A Revolution in History

Changes in the nature of history resulted from a major change in how we think about the past and how it is taught in most history courses. A generation or two ago, most introductory history courses in this country were more or less the same. They focused either on the development of **Western civilization** or on the history of the United States. They also concentrated on politics, war, and, to a lesser extent, philosophy and religion.

Then, there was a revolution in the way we view the past. There is now much greater emphasis on the roles of various cultures. Courses in American history now are much more likely to consider the role of Native Americans, African Americans, and immigrants from Asia and

Eastern and Southern Europe. Western civilization courses must take into consideration the contribution of Asian, African, and Native American peoples to human development. And, in many cases, traditional Western civilization courses have been replaced altogether by new **world civilization** courses, which focus on all of humanity.

New Subjects for History   The revolution in history did not involve just including more cultures to study. There also was a major change in *how* these cultures are studied. No longer is history simply the story of kings and popes, presidents and generals. Now everyone who has ever lived is fair game for the historian—rich or poor, powerful or powerless, male or female. And, history no longer is just about politics and public life. The private lives of ordinary people are now studied with the same care as the public actions of a Lincoln or a Napoleon.

This change is reflected in the way that history is taught. The table of contents of a current and popular world civilization textbook includes subheadings such as "Marriage and the Family," "The Status of Women," "Sexual Customs," "Education, Literacy, and the Printed Word," and "Poverty, Crime, and Social Control."[1] Not one of these topics would have been included in most textbooks 25 years ago. Today, however, they are all respected areas of study.

■

Personal Learning Questions
Think about the kinds of history covered in your course. What interests you most? What might you learn from a particular kind of history that might be useful to you in the future?

■

The Challenge Today   This expansion in the scope of history offers you great opportunities. The new history can be much more exciting and much more relevant to your own concerns. Learning how ordinary people faced economic crises in the past may, for example, be more useful to you than memorizing the details of a peace treaty. In your years as a student, you may, in fact, want to take courses from historians with a number of approaches. This way you can sample different "dishes" from the banquet history has to offer.

---

[1]Richard L. Greaves, Robert Zaller, Philip V. Cannistraro, and Rhoads Murphey, *Civilizations of the World*, Vol. II (New York: Harper and Row, 1990), p. vii.

However, this expansion of history also makes your task as a student more complicated. In the past, everyone had more or less the same idea of what was important in history. Now, one instructor may prefer to focus on the "meat and potatoes" of traditional history: the actions of political leaders, generals, and diplomats. Another instructor may devote a great deal of attention to groups—such as women, minorities, or the poor—that were generally ignored by earlier generations of historians. A third instructor may organize a course around a single issue, such as the changing nature of cities.

It is very important for you to adjust to the particular kind of history being presented. Some students don't understand this. They hold to their own notion of what history must be, and they ignore what their instructor is trying to teach. Their instructor lectures for an hour on the situation of women, but the students don't take notes. They are still waiting to hear "real history" when the lecture ends. What such students do not understand is that this information is real history. Moreover, it may be crucial for the next test.

POLITICS, WAR, AND DIPLOMACY

As you have learned, there are a number of different kinds of history, and all of them are legitimate. You may encounter any of these kinds of history in your course. There are important differences between them, however, and this should affect the way that you study. Therefore, in the remainder of this chapter, we will consider some of the most common kinds of history and discuss how you can best deal with each.

One of the more common kinds of history focuses on politics, war, and diplomacy. These subjects do continue to play a major role in historical research, and you must be prepared to deal with these issues. In many classes, however, these issues will be approached in ways that may be new to you.

Combining the New and the Old

The first thing to remember is that you must pay attention to the particular way in which your instructor is approaching an issue, even when you think that you are familiar with the material. This was made painfully obvious to George, a student in a large class on European history. George had been a military buff in high school and felt confident about the section on the First World War in his European history course. In fact, he actually knew more details about the strategies and tactics used in the war than his instructor.

On the exam, however, George found questions about the psychological appeal of propaganda and the role of women in the economy during the war. He was completely unprepared to answer these questions because he had ignored the material on the home front covered in the lectures and the readings. For most contemporary historians, though, this material is at least as important as the details of battles, and George's instructor expected him to learn it.

This same pattern can be found in many aspects of traditional history. **Political history** once focused almost entirely on the decisions of elite leaders. Now it may take into consideration the nature of political rallies or the role of the mass media. In the past, **military history** generally focused on the strategies of military leaders. Increasingly, however, it includes such topics as the impact of war on the average person. **Diplomatic history** was once the history of negotiations and treaties. Now it is just as likely to involve the ways that leaders use foreign affairs to strengthen their position at home. If you ignore these newer issues, you may not do as well in the course. Therefore, even in courses that focus on traditional topics, it is wise to keep an open mind concerning what counts as history.

The Role of Memorization

You may have come to view political, military, and diplomatic history as a matter of memorizing dates and facts. There is no question that in courses that emphasize these topics, it will be necessary to learn the dates of wars, revolutions, elections, and other major events. You will also need to commit to memory the positions of the major political figures or parties and the chief provisions of the most important treaties.

It is very important, however, to recognize that you rarely can do well in a college history course just by memorizing the textbook. There is simply too much information for most human beings to remember. You therefore must be very selective in deciding which dates and facts are most important.

Even if you could remember everything in the textbook, it would not be enough to guarantee success in the course. To operate on the college level, you must go beyond memorization. You will be expected to be able to use facts and dates, not just recall them. You will need to know, of course, *when* a particular war ended. However, it may be even more important to understand *how* the end of the war reshaped diplomacy, politics, and social and economic patterns. You will need to understand not only *what* positions a particular political party championed, but also *why* certain groups in society found it desirable to support that party. You will, in short, need to move beyond remembering facts toward interpreting these facts.

The Question of Perspective

In studying political, military, and diplomatic history, you will need to learn not only what happened but also how different groups viewed these happenings. The outbreak of a war, the election of a president, the signing of a treaty—each of these events meant different things to different people.

Thus, if you are studying the Dred Scott decision, which was handed down before the American Civil War, it is not enough to memorize the date it occurred. It is not even enough to know that in this case, the Supreme Court ruled that African Americans were not citizens. You must also understand what it *meant* to various groups. How would a Northern abolitionist be apt to view this decision? How would his or her view differ from that of a typical Southern plantation owner? How might a freed slave react to this decision?

To answer these questions, you will need to put yourself in the position of various groups of people. This requires a combination of knowledge and imagination. You will need to learn as much as possible about the lifestyles, education, values, and economic interests of particular groups. Then you will have to imagine how these factors might have shaped their reactions to events.

■

PERSONAL LEARNING QUESTIONS

How has putting yourself in the place of others helped you in the past? How might it help you in the future?

■

INTELLECTUAL AND CULTURAL HISTORY

In addition to political, military, and diplomatic history, many courses examine the ideas and the culture of earlier periods.[2] Some upper-level courses focus entirely on this area. Therefore, you will need to know how to succeed in it.

---

[2]The term *cultural history* is currently used two different ways. Traditionally, cultural history has meant the study of high culture in the past—the history, for example, of painting and literature. Increasingly, the word *cultural* is being used as it might be used in anthropology. In this case, cultural history would indicate the study of the cultural patterns of a society in the past, such as its responses to crime. In this section, the term will be used in its traditional sense.

Schools, Styles, and Movements

Intellectual history and **cultural history** are generally organized around schools, styles, or movements of thinkers or artists who shared some common perspective. The first step in dealing with such material is to create a general mental picture of each group. If, for example, you were learning about a movement such as the **Renaissance,** you would want to be able to answer questions such as the following: When did the Renaissance begin and when did it end? In what countries was it most prominent? Who were the most important artists and intellectuals associated with it? What ideas and artistic styles did it support?

The next step is to flesh out this general picture. You would need to fix in your mind a few specific works of art from the Renaissance that you could use as examples. In addition, you would need to know some of the specific ideas put forward by thinkers in this period. You also would want to become aware of differences within the movement. You would, for example, probably be expected to understand the differences between the art and ideas of the Italian Renaissance and those of the Renaissance in Northern Europe.

Once you have in mind a good working description of the style or movement, you can begin to compare it with others. Continuing our earlier example, you might want to contrast the art and ideas of the Renaissance with those of the **Middle Ages.** You might ask yourself what characteristics would distinguish a piece of medieval sculpture from a work by a Renaissance sculptor, such as Donatello or Michelangelo. What differences would you expect to find between a religious writer in the Middle Ages, such as St. Thomas Aquinas, and a secular writer in the Renaissance, such as Machiavelli?

Answering questions such as these will give you the "big picture" you need to understand these movements. If you are assigned original readings from the period or are shown examples of its art, try to determine how each may be seen as an example of the general patterns you have defined.

Assumptions and Values

If your course covers intellectual and cultural history in any depth, you probably will need to go beyond this framework. You will have to understand what the intellectuals and writers assumed about the world and what they thought was good and bad. In the case of the Renaissance, your basic framework might include the information that artists in this period glorified the human body. Now, you will have to go deeper and learn that they did so because they were **humanists,** people who believed that "man was the measure of all things."

Doing this effectively requires a certain empathy. You will need to put yourself in the place of artists and intellectuals of the period. You will have to imagine how the world would look from their perspective. You also will have to understand their fears and their desires.

This search for assumptions and values is particularly important when you read primary sources. This is not clear to many students. When they are presented with a source such as a **Puritan** sermon from colonial New England, they read it the same way they read their textbook. If the minister who wrote the sermon denounces the sin and debauchery of the local community, students assume that life was rather wild in early New England. What they do not realize is that their instructor put these readings on the syllabus to help them understand *how a Puritan minister viewed the world.* The point is that the minister assumed that there was sin everywhere, not that his congregation was actually so awful.

Understanding the Context

In the process of "getting into" the mind of the artist or intellectual, you also will have to consider the context within which he or she worked. A painting or a work of philosophy does not burst into being from nothing. It is always based on the experiences of its creator, and these experiences are shaped by the history of the period.

Thus, to fully understand how particular works came into being, you will have to understand the world that created them. What was the life of an artist or intellectual like in the period you are studying? How did the conditions of this life shape the nature of cultural and intellectual life? What ideas—religious or philosophical beliefs—inspired the works of the time? How did artists and intellectuals support themselves financially? How did this affect the nature of their work?

Such a reconstruction of the lives and environments of the intellectual and cultural figures of the past can help prepare you for an exam. At the same time, it can make the material you are reading much more interesting.

Using a Work of Art in a History Course

In courses that include intellectual and cultural history, you often will be expected to link specific works of art or expressions of ideas to other historical material. Some students find this to be a challenge. Therefore, let us go through the process in some detail.

Imagine that you are taking a European history course in which the instructor shows a slide of the Pablo Picasso painting *Guernica*. (See opposite.) The first step is simply to spend a little time looking at the work and learning to "see" it. You do not need to be a sophisticated art critic. Just pay attention to the subject matter (people in pain, confusion, and destruction) and to the style (rejection of traditional Western perspective, juxtaposition of planes at unexpected angles, mask shapes imitative of African art).

Then, try to relate what you see to what you have learned in the course. If you have already learned that Picasso's style of painting is known as **cubism,** look in the index of your textbook for the entries "Picasso," "Cubism," and "*Guernica*." Also go back over the class lectures to find ways that you can connect this particular painting to issues raised by your instructor. You may find a lecture about the way that modern artists in the early twentieth century abandoned Western traditions of art and looked to so-called primitive art for inspiration. Another lecture or a section in the textbook may refer to the horror with which intellectuals in the 1930s responded to the bombing of cities. Somewhere else you may find material on the **Spanish Civil War** and the responses of intellectuals to the conflict.

At this point you might want to draw a diagram. Place the name *Guernica* in the center of the diagram. Then, draw lines to connect it to related historical events. Now you are prepared to use *Guernica* as an example of a number of trends in modern European history. Here are some of the situations in which this painting might be of assistance.

1. You are faced with an exam question about the nature of modern art. *Guernica* can provide you with the perfect example of the cubist movement. Or, you might use it more generally to describe the breakdown of traditional ideas of perspective in Western painting.

2. During a discussion, you are called on to comment on European attitudes to non-Western peoples. You immediately think of the way Picasso painted patterns borrowed from African masks, and you use this as an example of a new respect for other cultures.

3. You are preparing for an essay exam, and you are almost sure that there will be a question on the impact of twentieth-century warfare on civilian populations. You remember that Picasso

Guernica, by Pablo Picasso

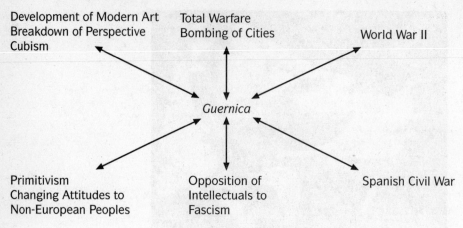

Development of Modern Art
Breakdown of Perspective
Cubism

Total Warfare
Bombing of Cities

World War II

Guernica

Primitivism
Changing Attitudes to
Non-European Peoples

Opposition of
Intellectuals to
Fascism

Spanish Civil War

A word diagram for *Guernica*

painted this painting after German planes bombed the Spanish city of *Guernica*. This was one of the first examples of aerial bombing against civilian targets, and it created an enormous scandal. You can begin with this event and the response to it, and then move on to discuss the blitz against London, the fire-bombing of Hamburg and Dresden, and the use of atomic bombs against Hiroshima and Nagasaki.

4. You are writing a short paper and need an example of the response to fascism in the 1930s. Once again, *Guernica* provides the perfect example. Picasso created the painting to alert the world to the threat of Nazi Germany and fascist Italy.

Thus, a few moments spent contemplating this painting and its connections to the issues of the course can be helpful in many contexts. Used effectively, this painting could in each case demonstrate your understanding of the material. Moreover, someday you may find yourself standing in front of this formidable work in a museum in Madrid and be glad that you can fully experience its power. And, even if you never make that trip to Spain, you may find that this work has opened up perspectives on the nature of modern warfare that will be valuable in learning to live in this world.

The Ideas and Culture of the People

In the preceding examples, we have considered elite culture—that is, works produced by professional artists and intellectuals and intended primarily for a minority of highly cultured people. However, the ideas and the art of everyday people also play a major role in contemporary history. Thus, you may find yourself studying popular religious cults of the ancient world, the oral traditions of an African village, or the role of rock and roll in the turmoil of the 1960s.

In dealing with such phenomena of folk or **popular culture,** you no longer will focus on the works of a few major artists or intellectuals. Instead, you will consider how particular kinds of art or ideas express or shape the values and attitudes of a broad segment of the population. Ask yourself what such works assume about the nature of human beings or about the world in general. What kinds of messages do they send about how human beings should act or about how society should be organized?

Whether you are studying Michelangelo or the Beatles, the Buddha or a revivalist preacher, intellectual and cultural history can add excitement to a course. It can make the past seem more real by helping you understand what was going on in the minds of the people you study.

■

Personal Learning Questions

When you look at a piece of art, do you wonder about the life of the artist? Are you curious about the events and situations that influenced the artist to create that piece of art?

■

SOCIAL HISTORY

As has already been suggested in the discussion of popular culture, historians have realized that the past is not just about the deeds of great men. Today, a great deal of historical research is devoted to reconstructing of the lives of ordinary people. Thus, you probably will encounter in your course some form of **social history**—the study of broader society in the past. Your instructor may, in fact, consider it the core of the course.

The History of Social Classes

In studying the lives of ordinary people, historians often focus on social classes. A **social class** is a large group of individuals who have similar occupations or means of earning a living. Slaves, **peasants,** industrial workers, **aristocrats,** the lower-middle class, and the middle class are common examples of such groups you will encounter in history courses. (See page 28, Understanding a Social Class from the Inside)

It is assumed that, as a group, the members of a class will tend to share certain common values and attitudes and to act in a similar manner. Of course, not all of the peasants in a particular period will act or view the world in precisely the same manner. However, it is argued, most of them will have more in common with each other than they will with aristocrats.

Viewed from this perspective, much previous history may be seen as conflict between different social classes. Most probably, you will study the struggles between the wealthy classes and the poor classes. Common examples of this include the battles between **plebeians** and **patricians** in the ancient world, between peasants (**serfs**) and aristocrats in the Middle Ages, between aristocrats and commoners in early-modern Europe, between workers (**proletariat**) and the middle class (**bourgeoisie**) in industrialized societies, and between landholders and peasants in many areas of the Third World today. Sometimes, though, class struggle is between two wealthy classes that use different ways to gain wealth. Examples of this are conflicts between aristocrats and the middle class and conflicts between Southern plantation owners and Northern industrialists during the **Industrial Revolution.**

The notion of social class has been subjected to many attacks from those who believe that it oversimplifies history. It remains, however, one of the most common tools of historical analysis. Thus, you will need to understand the nature of each major class in the period you are studying. You will need to develop a clear picture of the interests, perspectives, and actions of the members of each group. You must, once again, go beyond memorizing the definitions in the textbook and learn to understand a social class from the inside. Through this process you can gain a real understanding of the material, which will help you not only in this particular course but also in dealing with other groups you encounter in your own life.

The History of Everyday Life, Family, and the Life Cycle

In recent decades, historians have become increasingly fascinated with the daily lives of ordinary people. At one end of the spectrum, they have begun to explore the larger framework within which people conducted their lives. They have asked questions such as how did economic changes, technological innovations, and population shifts change everyday existence? How has human life been affected by migrations, disease, climate, and the environment?

At the other extreme, historians have begun to explore the details of ordinary life. What did people eat? What were their houses like? Where and how did they do their work? How did they spend their leisure time? Issues that would have been ignored by earlier historians are now studied in detail. A village festival or a World Fair, for example, may be just as interesting as an election or a treaty.

One of the areas that has received a great deal of attention is the family. In the past, the family was seen as part of the unchanging backdrop to real history. Now, historians recognize that the family has undergone changes as complex and varied as any other aspect of human life. There have been revolutions in the size and definition of families, just as there have been revolutions in politics. And, the roles of family members have changed from period to period, as has the role of families in the broader society.

Along with family history came studies of the life cycle. Historians discovered that the definition of childhood has changed over time. They suggest that adolescence may be a modern invention and that old age may have meant different things in different periods. Even the experience of death has became a subject of history.

The Poor and the Oppressed

Traditional history generally focused on the elites of past societies and ignored the poor, the oppressed, and racial minorities. During the past 25 years, however, historians have worked to reclaim the history of these groups. The first step was to search for previously ignored artists, writers, and political leaders from those segments of the population that had not been included in history. Historians soon realized that most people in these groups had not been allowed to play an active role in public life or to record their thoughts for future generations.

Therefore, historians began to explore new ways of understanding the experiences of poor, oppressed, or minority communities. Perhaps the most impressive job of recapturing these lost voices has been in the field of pre-Civil War African American history. Historians have used the diaries of escaped slaves, plantation records, and oral traditions to reconstruct the experience of slaves. The result has been a revolution in our image of the slave system. We have become increasingly aware of the spirited and subtle resistance of early African Americans to their control by slave owners.

UNDERSTANDING A SOCIAL CLASS FROM THE INSIDE

Think about what it must have been like to be a slave in ancient Rome, a medieval peasant, a nineteenth-century factory worker, or a member of whatever social class you are studying. What would your life experiences have been like? What sort of family, education, and expectations for the future would you have? What would you be apt to know about and not know about in the society of your time? What would you be most concerned about on a daily basis?

Once you have a least a partial image of life within this social class, move to another group and repeat the process. Then, begin to imagine an encounter between members of the two groups. Where would they disagree? How would each tend to view the other? How would each react to the major events or issues of the time?

Many of the same methods now have been used for researching in virtually all periods and nations. The lives of slaves, peasants, factory workers, racial and ethnic minorities, and other oppressed groups have become a part of history. In the process, historians have been forced to redefine their notions of power. No longer is power seen as simply a matter of laws and armies and police. It now is recognized that almost any social institution can be used to maintain inequality. Prisons, school systems, advertising techniques, and anthropological theory have all become a part of the history of oppression.

■

PERSONAL LEARNING QUESTIONS

How has the social class into which you were born influenced your life up to this point? How can understanding your own social history help you to understand yourself?

■

WOMEN AND GENDER STUDIES

The Growth of Women's History

As we have seen, historians in recent decades have devoted enormous energy to understanding the lives of those who had been left out of traditional history. One of the most significant effects of this has been the realization that traditional history systematically ignored the role of half the human race. The impact of feminism since the late 1960s has encouraged historians to change this. Important female artists, writers, thinkers, and political figures of the past now are given the recognition they deserve.

At the same time, the development of new forms of social history has opened up new possibilities in women's history. Traditional history generally focused on areas, such as war and politics, from which most women were excluded. Social history, however, has tended to focus our attention on everyday life. Here, it became obvious that the lives of women are every bit as important as those of their male counterparts.

In the process, it was realized that women do in fact have a history. In the past, it was a commonly held belief that the roles and activities of women were determined by biology and, thus, did not change. When social historians reexamined the past, however, they discovered that the lives of women had changed as much as those of men.

Sex and Gender

To understand this new social history of women, it is necessary to grasp the distinction between sex and **gender.** Sex is a biological category, in most cases determined by the presence or absence of a Y chromosome. The difference between typical male and female genitals is a prime example of a sexual difference.

Gender, by contrast, is a social category. In every society, girls and boys, women and men are taught to behave in certain ways. They learn to act and to be treated in certain ways. This entire complex of culturally determined behavior and perspectives is called *gender.*

Sexual differences are roughly the same in all cultures and in all periods. Gender differences, by contrast, change like any other historical phenomenon. One of the great contributions of women's history has been to make us realize how many of the differences we once attributed to biology are in fact gender differences.

The History of Gender

A significant amount of research has been devoted to the history of women's role and experiences. We now know a great deal about how women lived, thought, and acted in earlier eras. This material may play a very important role in any history course you take.

Gender, however, is not simply a female phenomenon. The thoughts and actions of men are also shaped by the way gender is defined in particular eras. Historians have not yet devoted as much research to the impact of gender roles on men as on women. The study of such roles is a growing field, however, and thus your history course may include the history of men, as well as the history of women.

■

PERSONAL LEARNING QUESTION

How can understanding the difference between sex and gender help you to understand the opposite sex?

■

THE ABUNDANCE OF HISTORY

Identifying What Is Most Important in Your History Course

No instructor can deal in depth with all aspects of history in a single course. Because of this, he or she must make decisions concerning which aspects of history to emphasize. Therefore, one of your first tasks in taking a history course is to determine what kinds of history are being stressed. As you have learned, the syllabus is a good place to begin. In addition, subject headings that accompany the readings may give you a good idea of what is most important to your instructor. If your textbook devotes a great deal of space to social history and you have been assigned to read a novel that depicts the lives of everyday people, you can bet that your instructor considers social history to be important.

Pay attention to what is stressed in lectures. If possible, find out what kinds of questions were used on old exams. In addition, you almost always can approach your instructor during office hours to ask what aspects of history are most important in this course.

All of this should give you a good idea of what is important early in the semester. Stay alert, though. Your instructor may stress certain aspects of history early in the semester, and others later on. What was important to study for the first exam may be less important on the final exam.

What's in it for You?

The creation of new kinds of history may leave some students wishing they were back in the days when historians spent most of their time on war and politics. Keep in mind, though, this expansion of history opens up extraordinary possibilities.

Very few students who studied the traditional history curriculum ever went on to be elected president, sign a treaty, or lead an army in battle. In contrast, many students will someday find themselves having to deal with precisely the kinds of issues discussed in contemporary history classes. How have ordinary people in the past responded to economic upheavals or political chaos? How have issues of gender and sexuality been dealt with in the past? How have various racial or ethnic groups succeeded or failed in their efforts to live with one another? Answering questions like these can be enormously useful to you.

Perhaps most important, the new history can help you learn to see the world through the eyes of someone who has had a very different set of life experiences. Studying the past, as contemporary historians do, can give you access to a wide variety of life experiences. Each perspective has something crucial to offer to you.

Moreover, the new history provides greater possibilities for enjoyment. In most courses, one still can identify with the great leaders and live their lives. There is, however, something fascinating about learning what objects were in a peasant's home, how slaves learned to play mental games on their masters, or what nineteenth-century doctors believed to be signs of sexual dysfunction in women. The instructors in your history courses will probably be offering you a much richer set of experiences than those encountered by earlier generations of history students.

■

PERSONAL LEARNING QUESTIONS

What can you gain from the particular subject matter in this course? How might it help you in future life?

■

APPLICATION EXERCISES

1. What ideas about history did you bring to your current course?

2. How was history taught in your elementary, middle, and high schools? To what extent had the "revolution" in history affected those courses?

3. How has the nature of typical introductory history courses changed?

4. What kinds of topics, once ignored, are now covered in history courses?

5. What ideas about the subject matter of history did you bring to your current course? What groups of people in the past did you think historians study? How many of the following topics did you expect to find in a history course?

    Politics
    War
    Diplomacy
    Artistic and intellectual movements
    Popular culture
    Daily life in other periods
    Social classes
    Racial and ethnic minorities
    Women
    Children
    Sexuality and gender

6. What aspects of history do you think are most important in the course you are currently taking? How can you determine what is most important to your instructor? Which aspects of contemporary history has your instructor stressed? Which are deemphasized?

7. What basic concepts seem crucial in your course? Is social class important in this course? Does the concept of gender play a major role? Are there other basic organizing concepts in the course?

TERMS TO KNOW

aristocrats	patricians
bourgeoisie	peasants
contemporary	plebeians
cubism	political history
culture	popular culture
cultural history	proletariat
diplomatic history	Puritan
gender	Renaissance

humanists
Industrial Revolution
intellectual history
Middle Ages
military history
Pablo Picasso

serfs
social history
social class
Spanish Civil War
Western civilization
world civilization

CHAPTER 3

MANAGING YOUR ENERGY, TIME, AND MIND

GETTING FOCUSED

- *How are you going to respond to the challenges of the history course you are taking?*

- *How are you going to summon the energy needed to do well? How are you going to organize your time to make sure that you are able to study?*

- *How are you going to develop effective study strategies to ensure that you get the maximum benefit from every minute you devote to your history course?*

- *How do you think about time? Do you think of it as a commodity, something you can buy, spend, invest, waste, or borrow? Or, do you think of time as an agent, something that can stand still, not wait, heal wounds, or be on your side?*

- *Think of a day when you were able to accomplish a great number of tasks and goals. What factors were operating in the way you worked that made the day productive?*

- *Think of a day when you weren't able to accomplish half as much as you usually do. What was going on that interfered with your efficiency?*

MOTIVATION: FINDING YOUR OWN ENERGY

Human beings need energy to do work. Learning is work and therefore requires energy. It is worth stopping a moment to think about where you will get the energy you need for success in your history course.

In addition to food and rest, **motivation** is an important source of human energy. First, there is something you want. Then, energy appears so that you can do what you need to do to get it. In some situations, new learning is "what you need to do" to reach a desired goal. In other situations, it emerges out of a desire to satisfy your curiosity. In either case, true learning is never passive. It is not something done to you. It is something that *you* do in order to achieve certain goals.

Defining Your Goals

Because true learning is always a response to specific goals, it is time to define your goals. Before you begin specifying goals for your history course, look at the reasons that you are in college in the first place. Stop for a moment and do an inventory of the reasons why you are investing the time and money it takes to complete a college degree.

Consider the following reasons for being in college and rank their importance to you:

Reason	Very Important	Somewhat Important	Not Important
Expectations of family, friends, etc.			
Desire for a degree			
Personal knowledge & growth			
Social development			
Career opportunity			
Other			

If you find, as many students do, that you have a clearer idea of other people's expectations for you than of your own expectations for yourself, stop and think about what you are doing. It takes a great deal of energy to do well in college, and it is difficult to find that energy if you are doing it all for someone else. Identify your own personal reasons for getting a college education. If you really get in touch with your own desire, you can tap into that rich vein of energy within yourself.

Even having a general goal of graduation from college is not enough. You also need to have specific goals for each course. We say "goals" because there may be many things you can achieve through taking a particular course. Even if you are taking a course simply because it is required, you can take advantage of the opportunity and achieve other goals at the same time.

So, what goals might you have for your history course? Your goals may be quite practical, such as earning a diploma so that you can go on to seek other goals in life. They may be cultural, such as preparing for future travel to other countries. They may be intellectual, such as gaining a broad base of information or learning to think critically. Or, you may be motivated simply by the pure pleasure of learning something new.

The Pitfall of "Learned Helplessness"

True learning is always associated with empowerment. You must feel a certain sense of mastery in order to learn effectively, and all true learning increases your sense of personal power in some fashion. Such a sense of mastery, though, is not always easy to maintain. All of us have had our failures, and we all have received criticism from those around us. In the face of this, it is easy to become convinced that there is no reason to try to achieve, that the best we can do is just survive what fate has to throw at us. Be aware, however, that this state of mind can lead to passivity and dependence.

Such **learned helplessness** can feed on itself, as each withdrawal from life produces a new failure, and each failure drives the individual deeper into withdrawal. When you view other people in this state of mind, you probably realize that there is a lot they could do to help themselves. They, however, are not able to see these alternatives, or they don't have the energy or self-confidence to try them.

Such a mental state is not helpful in the classroom. Learning becomes an ordeal. It is experienced as something inflicted from the outside, something beyond one's control. The sense of helplessness saps energy and keeps the student from distinguishing between successful and unsuccessful strategies. Such a student may actually invest a good deal of energy in a course, but this investment is not apt to yield major rewards because real learning involves a constant feedback process and that, in turn, assumes an active relationship with the classroom environment.

The good news, however, is that learned helplessness is just that: learned. What has been learned can be unlearned. Once you begin to recognize that there is an alternative to helplessness, you cease to be a victim. In the remainder of this book, we will provide concrete steps by which you can redefine your relationship to history and become empowered in your classes. We will break up the large challenges facing you into manageable units, and then offer you ways to master each small piece of the whole.

Motivation as a Resource for Learning

If you sometimes fall into this victim role, the first step towards overcoming it is to get in touch with your own goals and see how they relate to the course you are taking. Motivation is a necessary prerequisite to any kind of voluntary activity. You can breathe and pump blood without deciding to, but your academic learning will emerge only from a long-term commitment. Even the most interesting class will contain material that seems tedious. Learning to comprehend new concepts is a gradual process, like learning to play a new instrument or game, and there may be a long wait before you feel that you are really getting the hang of it. Remember that even the most fortunate student careers contain some courses that are unforgivably boring or crushingly difficult. Only if you remain in constant touch with a strong sense of motivation will you have the resources of energy to make it successfully through the deserts and the jungles of your college years.

How, precisely, can you go about finding your motivation? This question must be approached on two levels. First, what is your motivation for being in college in the first place? In some cases, the answer to this question may be more difficult than you expect. All through your life, other people have been giving you good reasons for going to college. However, if you have not yet made those reasons your own, then perhaps you have no reason to be there.

It may be a good idea, therefore, to stop and do an inventory of possible justifications for the time and expense of a college education and see which ones really touch your life. If you cannot find good reasons to continue, then you should at least consider leaving for a while. The freedom to choose whether you stay or leave may help you get in touch with your own desire for a college education, a desire which may have been smothered in the expectations of others.

Of course, you can't just be in college. You have to have a course of study, a program that will include at least one major field of concentration and probably one or more minors. This program should reflect your broader motivations and goals. Even if you have not selected a major field—and there's nothing wrong with "playing the field" until you are certain what exactly you want—it is essential that you frame some sort of general goals that will serve to guide your experiments.

Once you have determined that you do want to remain in school—and we assume that you do, since you're still reading this book—you need to think about what motivations you have for the particular history course in which you are enrolled. If possible, talk to students whom you respect and who have already taken courses from particular instructors, and ask these students what they gained from their courses. Ask yourself what you might gain from taking this course. The fulfillment of certain requirements? A particular grade? Skills that will be useful in later life? Knowledge about some period of history or aspect of life that makes you curious? Greater cultural sophistication? Preparation for future travel? A sense of accomplishment? A challenge to explore possibilities that haven't even occurred to you yet?

Make a list of all the things you might like to get out of this class. Return to this list periodically throughout the semester to remind yourself that the course is a means through which you can achieve *your* goals. Remember, even if your primary reason for taking a course is to fulfill a requirement, it is going to take a significant amount of your time in the next several months. You might as well get something back from your investment in addition to a grade on a transcript. The more extras you can get back from each course, the richer your life will be.

Throughout the semester, add to the list of what you expect to get from the course. When it becomes clear that particular goals are not being achieved, try to imagine ways that you might be able to get these things. Sometimes you will find that your goals were unreasonable. Sometimes you will feel that a particular course failed to live up to what you could reasonably expect of it. In any case, you will know that this is *your* college education and that you are actively involved in shaping and evaluating your fate. And, you will probably find new sources of energy driving your studies.

■

PERSONAL LEARNING QUESTIONS

What are your primary reasons for being in college? How can you further these goals this semester?
What was your primary reason for signing up for your history course? What other things might you get out of it?

■

Energy: The Physical Side of Success in History

Motivation is not simply a mental phenomenon. It requires energy as well as determination, and the amount of energy that you have at your disposal depends, to a great extent, on the condition of your body.

Energy is a physical commodity. You manufacture it from raw materials such as food, rest, and exercise. Your brain burns up a large percentage of it, and there are certain nutrients that are especially useful to the brain. Because the brain makes heavy use of protein, adequate sources of this nutrient are necessary to sustain mental activity. It has been suggested that choline, of which eggs, soybeans, and liver are good sources, enhances memory. This occurs, presumably, because choline becomes acetylcholine, a chemical transmitter that activates nerve impulses across the synapse, or electrical connection between one neuron and another.

Conversely, there seems to be strong evidence that heavy consumption of sugar, which overstimulates the pancreas and causes a drop in blood sugar, weakens the physical basis for forming and retrieving memories. Literature on nutrition is worth consulting to gain a better understanding of the role that various foods, vitamins, and minerals play in the functioning of the brain. It will also be helpful for you to know the idiosyncrasies of your body, such as your reactions to particular foods, tolerance of sugar, rate of metabolism, and reactions to stimulants such as caffeine, since your body's responses may differ from the responses of others.

Sleep is another crucial element in determining how much energy you have available to achieve your goals. You probably can get by with far less than eight hours a night, but is "getting by" what you really want? Staggering into an exam, bleary-eyed and fuzzy in the head, may mean that the previous weeks of studying will earn a full letter grade less than it would have if you had been alert. And, two hours of studying while suffering from sleep deprivation may not accomplish as much as a few minutes spent under better conditions. Getting whatever amount of sleep your body needs can be a real challenge in many college environments, but becoming master of one's sleep schedule is one of the most important aspects of success.

It also may be wise to pay attention to your sleep patterns and their relationship to your work. In 1924, two researchers named Jenkins and Dallenbach found that sleep *following* study will help memory, but sleep just *before* study may interfere with it. (This effect was found to apply to sleep periods of four hours or less, rather than to a full night's sleep.) The researchers suggest that sleeping for short periods before studying interferes with memory because the body produces high levels of the hormone somatrophin during the early and middle stages of sleep. This hormone can adversely affect the formation of memories. Thus, if you only have a short time to sleep, you should sleep *after* you study rather than *before* you study.

Exercise can be another important component in your preparation for academic success. Your brain is a physical organ susceptible to the physiological changes induced by activity, especially weight-bearing exercise such as walking, running, or playing tennis. For many, vigorous physical activity may be a necessary complement to intense mental activity, for both physical and psychological reasons. It can reduce the tension and toxins that accumulate in your body during long periods of sitting, thus allowing you to make much better use of the time you do spend studying.

Habits such as smoking, drinking, and taking other drugs can also limit the effectiveness of your study time. They can create stress in the body, reduce the resources you have to devote to your studies, and undercut your attempts to schedule. If you regularly use such substances, carefully observe their impact on your academic career. Imagine how the previous week or previous month might have been different if you had eliminated, or at least moderated, your intake. If you determine that the cost has been high, then you have a decision to make. Remember, learning to avoid being a victim in your academic work involves abandoning the victim role in other aspects of your life as well.

Emotions and Academic Success

As you probably are only too well aware, successful performance in your courses is not independent of your emotional state. Anxiety and other intense emotional states cause chemical changes in the brain. It has been suggested, for example, that a high level of anxiety, such as that experienced by people who have an extreme fear of tests, disrupts information processing. When faced with an anxiety-producing situation, the individual may switch from logical, sequential processing (thought to be governed largely by the left hemisphere of the brain) to a more emotional "fight or flight" response. This can paralyze the person's normal ability to call on memories and problem-solving skills.

One form of therapy that has helped people calm their anxiety is rational self-talk. Because language is itself a sequential and logical process, it can be used to lead one to a reasonable state of mind when faced with a cognitive task. Think about times when you found it helpful to talk to someone about an intensely emotional situation. The very act of using words and syntax to interpret the meaning of the problem can be therapeutic.

Emotion is not always, however, the foe of productive thinking. On the contrary, it is a necessary part of the process, as long as it doesn't get out of control. Animal studies, for example, have demonstrated the importance of adrenaline in learning. The release of adrenaline into the system is associated with instinctual responses, like the "fight or flight" reaction mentioned earlier. Thus, at some basic level, a charge of adrenaline signals importance. If the charge is not so great that it creates panic and short-circuits rational thought, it will add strong significance to an event and make it more memorable.[1] Of course, most of us are unlikely to experience strong surges of adrenaline while studying the decline of the Roman empire or the causes of the Industrial Revolution. But in the mild or moderate state of tension often experienced while preparing a paper or studying for a test, higher adrenaline levels enhance learning. This optimum level will occur, however, only if you carefully avoid circumstances that induce actual panic, such as waiting too long to begin.

Thus, your emotions may be either a tool for learning or an impediment, and you can have a great deal of control over which is most frequently the case. Pay attention to your emotional patterns and their relationship to your learning. What situations tend most often to produce a harmonious blend of emotions for studying? Which encourage unproductive tensions or anxieties? What changes in your life might make

---

[1]James R. McGaugh, "Adrenaline: A Secret Agent in Memory." *Psychology Today* 14:7 (December 1980), p. 132.

the positive experiences more frequent and the negative experiences less frequent?

If you continue to find that strong emotions hinder your work, take this as an important message that you have issues in your life that must be faced. The college years are a period of rapid change for most students, and you may need to deal directly with your emotional concerns. Sessions with a counselor or therapist or time spent each day exploring your feelings in a journal can help you clear up problems that otherwise might haunt you for decades. And, if you set aside a regular time to deal with strong feelings, either alone or with someone else, you will probably find that these emotions will be much less likely to hinder your academic success.

■

Personal Learning Questions

**How do the ways that you choose to treat your body affect
your studying, both positively and negatively?
In the past week, what have been your patterns of eating,
sleeping, exercising, smoking, drinking, or using other drugs?
Which do you think added to the effectiveness of your studying?
Which detracted from it?
Have your emotions been more of an ally or an enemy of your
studying in the past week? What steps can you take to gain
more harmony between your feelings and your academic goals?**

■

Gaining Mastery

The issues raised in this section may seem secondary, but in many cases these very factors make or break a student's academic career. If you are not sure whether you want to be in school or why you are taking a particular class, if you are not taking adequate control of your body or your emotions, this is apt to show up in your schoolwork sooner or later. If, on the other hand, you pay attention to the patterns of your life and make conscious choices as to how you want to live, you can lay a foundation for success that will go far beyond your college years and your professional activities.

Don't get discouraged if you cannot change the patterns of a lifetime in a weekend. Such alterations of your everyday life take time, and you may occasionally need help from others along the way. But, if you keep at it, if you remain conscious of the small choices you make each day and continue to try to make your life your own, the rewards will be enormous.

TIME MANAGEMENT

Time, like the earth, is a precious and finite resource to be managed as carefully as possible. **Time management** really is quite a simple concept. It combines the elements of *concentration* and *organization.* Concentration gives you the power to accomplish a task with minimum distraction. Organization frees you from indecisiveness so that you can maintain that concentration.

In studying for a history course, organization means scheduling your study and review time so that you can most effectively prepare for assignments and examinations. Concentration means making the best use of the time you have allotted.

■

PERSONAL LEARNING QUESTIONS

How successfully have you scheduled your time during the past year? Have you generally been prepared for exams and assignments or has your life been marked by a series of crises? What has worked for you when you tried to schedule in the past? What strategies would you like to try in the future?

■

Planning and Scheduling

As a student, you should use **three levels of planning:** semester-long planning, weekly planning, and daily planning. The semester-long planning will involve listing the exams and due dates for all your classes on a master calendar along with other activities and commitments that you know are forthcoming. Any calendar that provides a sizable space for each day will work. You might want to have this master calendar on a wall or other prominent place in your room. Be sure to add new items as they come along, so that you're never caught by surprise.

As you begin to work on your master calendar, ask yourself the following questions. What elements do I want to include? What are the major assignments and tests in my courses? How far ahead should I begin preparing for them? What major social events do I want to allot time for? Are there times when I can get ahead, so that I can have more freedom to choose when to have fun later?

Think of your weekly planning schedule as an enlargement of one component of your master calendar. On the weekend, take a few min-

Fall semester hadn't gone that well for Erin. She found herself always struggling to keep up with her assignments, studying late hours and cramming before exams. And, her grades had been markedly lower than what she was used to receiving in high school. So when she received a Sierra Club desk calendar for Christmas, Ann decided to use it to set up a three-level time management system. The calendar provided a two-page spread for each week: a beautiful photograph on one side, and the days marked in sections about an inch high and four inches wide. The picture was for aesthetic pleasure, something very important to Erin. The calendar page was for business. As soon as she had collected all her course syllabi, Erin sat down and entered every class, test, and due date she had available on each day's page. In this way, she was emulating a professional person whose day is regulated by appointments. She also purchased a small pad of lined sheets, each title "Things to Do Today," and stapled it inside the back cover of her calendar. With that, she was set. Each Sunday evening, she sat down and planned out the following week, noting on each day how she would spend her time. Throughout the week, she added new items as they came up. Each morning, she made a list of "Things to Do Today," and stapled it to the corner of the calendar page. As the week progressed, her stack of lists grew, so that at the end of the week she could compare her plans with her actual accomplishments. Over the semester, the calendar became a diary, accounting for her experiences and activities. By the end of the year, it was so full of valuable information that she kept it for future reference.

utes to sit down and think about your week to come. Then, sketch in on the calendar your study time for each class and your work time for each activity, paper, and project you must complete. This is the level of time management, by the way, that everyone thinks is a good idea and few people actually carry out. It is, however, an extremely powerful strategy for success.

To plan an effective weekly schedule, ask yourself how successful your time management was last week. How might more systematic planning and scheduling have allowed you to achieve your goals more effectively? Imagine the schedule that you wish you had created for yourself last week. How would this schedule have allowed you to improve your schoolwork and enjoy life at the same time?

It is true that you probably will need to revise your weekly schedule. Keep in mind, though, that the idea is not to write a script for yourself. Rather, it is to look at your week as a whole so that you can set priorities and ensure that the important tasks get done. Once you get in the habit of doing this, you will have a new sense of direction and control, which in turn will give you more confidence in everything you do.

Daily planning is the real script. On the evening before or the morning of each day, write down everything you need to do, from the most mundane to the most important. Put a star by those items that absolutely *must* be accomplished. Such a list, in the context of your weekly schedule, will give you an unfailing sense of purpose as you move through your day (and hopefully get at least half the items on your list done). As an example, here is Erin's initial list (boldface and underlines indicate subsequent highlighting of essential items).

Wednesday, February 23:

Composition (8:00)

History lecture (9:00—West Hall)

Psych lecture (11:00—Sheldon Hall)

Database search in library

Meet Sam for lunch (12:00—Commons)

Prof. Taylor appointment (2:30—West Hall)

Poster sale at Student Union

Study group review for history midterm (7:30)

Film "Raise the Red Lantern" at Auburn Hall (9:00)

Shirt sale at Emporium

Read chapter for biology Thurs.

Shopping: note cards, videotapes, yogurt, highlighters, shampoo, granola, hard pretzels

Order printer cartridges

Call Sarah about ride at spring break

Speaker on health care reform 4:00—West Hall

Math Help Clinic 8–11 P.M.

Writing Center: draft for Monday's assignment

Dinner

Erin decided that all previously made appointments and classes were essential. Also, reading the biology chapter for the next day was essential for the lecture to be comprehensible. These selections left a lot of items, probably too many to accomplish. Next, Erin organized these items around the essential commitments.

Composition (8:00)

History lecture (9:00)

Psych lecture (11:00)

Meet Sam for lunch (12:00—Commons)

Poster sale at Student Union

Pick up items at student store: note cards, videotapes, shampoo, hard pretzels, highlighters

Order printer cartridges

Prof. Taylor appointment (2:30—West Hall)

Database search in library

Speaker on health care reform 4:00—West Hall

Call Sarah about spring break ride

Dinner

Read chapter for biology Thurs.

Study group review for history midterm (7:30)

Film "Raise the Red Lantern" at Auburn Hall (9:00)

As you can see, Erin managed to fit in a pretty full day that balances studying, attending classes, and taking care of other matters. At the end of the day, a few items were left over to be rescheduled into another day's plans.

Writing Center: draft for Monday's assignment

Math Clinic

Buy yogurt and granola

In time, these too may become "essential items" and receive priority in Erin's planning.

The habit of planning does more than yield a productive day. It gives you control over both your short- and long-range future. After you learn to assess how you use your time (see the exercises at the end of this chapter), you can spot general trends and alter habits if you wish.

❦❦❦ FEBRUARY/MARCH ❦❦❦

Sun 27	Draft major thesis and outline for comp paper	3:00 Volleyball team practice 7:00 Fine Arts, film w/Jeff & Ann
Mon 28	8:00 Psych 10:00 History 11:00 Bio Lecture 1:00–5:00 Bio Lab	Lunch w/Jill *make appt. Financial Aid Office 7:00 Hayden Symph. Recital Hall w/Bill
Tues 1	10:00–11:00 French 12:00 Brown bag French Conversation/ Review See lab A1 2:30–3:45 Composition	4:30 Meet Joan at gym for running 7:00 History Study Group
Wed 2	8:00 Psych 10:00 History 11:00 Bio Lecture 3:30–5:30 History reading–Library	1:00–3:00 Review for French Test 8:00: Study French with Carla & Ron
Thur 3	10:00–11:45 FRENCH TEST 2:30–3:45 Composition: Bring draft for peer editing & Evening at Library hall 114	7:00 Time Management Workshop-Carver **Call home tonight for Mom's Birthday!!!!
Fri 4	8:00 Psych 10:00 History 11:00 Bio Lecture 1:00 Writing Lab	Afternoon: Campus Speak-Out for Multiculturalism Table: 2:00–4:00 ***Movie & Pizza w/Ron, Julie, and Eric***
Sat 5	Block-out morning for final revision–copy of comp on Library: Bib for history paper –10 items	Game?????

Making Strategic Use of Time

All people have "up" times and "down" times. Are you a "morning person" or a "night person?" Are you always sleepy at 3:00 in the afternoon? You probably know yourself and your **biorhythm patterns** quite well. This is information that should enter into your time management. If there are times when you know your brain shuts down 50 percent, either plan a nap to refresh yourself for later or do chores like the laundry or shopping that don't require the mental energy of studying. Try to avoid taking a difficult course or planning an intensive study session during that daily low period.

Another good strategy for using time is to relate study time to lectures. Reviewing just before or just after a lecture maximizes the value of both the lecture and your notes.

Toward the end of the year, after she had been keeping her time management system for two semesters and a summer, Erin decided to review how she had been using her time. She had been feeling a little let down by her college experience. Gradewise, she had done better since her first semester, but still she felt that she lacked a clear purpose. The time was coming to select a major, and she wasn't sure of her initial choice of business. Reviewing the calendar was like reviewing her life. She saw all the things she had done and even remembered quite often how she had felt—interested, frustrated, bored, or triumphant. As she examined her calendar, she realized that there were certain subjects that consistently brought up positive feelings. Certain other subjects had the opposite effect.

By paying attention to what truly interested and rewarded her, Erin formed a more personalized picture of her real priorities in life. She realized that she was strongly attracted to areas such as psychology, sociology, and history. Their common thread, it seemed, was their focus on understanding and helping people.

She decided to rethink her commitment to a major and look into such careers as health or education. The one biology course she tool had also been a positive experience. Now she planned to look into the requirements for a major in health counseling. Already feeling excited by this prospect, Erin could hardly wait to get her new Sierra Club calendar and begin to plan her year of purposeful involvement in her new goal.

Setting Priorities and Avoiding Procrastination

There isn't enough time in a day, of course, to do all you should or want to do. Time is your life, however, so how you choose to spend it is directly related to how your life turns out. Your weekly and daily planning reflect what you want out of your college career. Some people never think about that and, in the end, what they get may not be what they really wish they had.

One of the most common things that prevent us from matching our behavior to our goals is **procrastination.** As the most notorious thief of time, procrastination may be a habit you must confront. If you are putting off your reading, not beginning to review for tests in time, or stalling before tackling major projects, you are a procrastinator. The following advice, adapted from Jeffrey Mayer's book on time management,[2] may help you kick the procrastination habit:

Don't let yourself substitute a trivial task for an important one.

Doing your laundry or catching up on your social correspondence is not an acceptable substitute for getting started on that paper.

Give yourself a reward when you successfully overcome procrastination. If necessary, put the "price" of accomplishing a specific task on everything you want to do for fun. When you are in the habit of "earning" your free time, you will enjoy it much more.

If necessary, be stern with yourself. Imagine the worst possible outcome of not getting your work done: a low grade, a low GPA, failure to get into the major you desire, failure to be competitive in the job market later, etc. Let the "parent" in you speak sensibly to the "child."

Start big projects immediately. When you know you must write a paper, brainstorm for ideas, make a list of possible topics, and go to the library for a preliminary bibliography search. Start thinking about your midterm exams the first day of classes. Draw up a strategic plan to get things done well and on time.

Get and stay organized. Break down big tasks into smaller steps. Specific tasks that you know you can accomplish will not tempt you to procrastinate as much as large tasks that seem vague to you.

---

[2]Jeffrey Mayer, *If you Haven't Got the Time to Do It Right, When Will You Find the Time to Do It Over?* (New York: Simon and Schuster, 1990).

The Art of Taking Breaks

You are not a machine, and no matter how efficiently you plan your time, you won't go nonstop from morning to night (unless perhaps you really are under pressure and then only for brief periods). Lapses of attention and interruptions are natural occurrences. However, you can exert control. Because your mind is almost certain to wander when you try to concentrate on the same thing for a long period, it is reasonable to vary tasks. Try to follow a rhythm of your own in keeping with your normal attention span. Again, you know yourself best. Stop regularly to summarize what you have been studying, and be sure that you master the "art of taking breaks."

Breaks can be necessary to the successful study session. They let your newly acquired knowledge sink in. They prevent you from becoming hypnotized or sleepy. They enable you to rest your eyes, stir up your circulation, and nourish yourself if that's needed. Breaks can serve as rewards, which motivate you to persevere, or as tactical moments to decide whether or not you should change tasks.

This assumes, however, that you are controlling your breaks and not vice versa. You might decide in advance how much you will accomplish before taking a break. And, when you have reached that point, prepare for coming back. If it is a break in reading, summarize what you've read thus far as preparation for continuing later. If you are writing, you may write the first sentence of the next paragraph to help you start up again. Keep breaks short, so that you are back on task before your short-term memory begins to erase what you've just done.

Even with regular breaks, you may find that during study your mind wanders and your body becomes fidgety. When a task becomes difficult, confusing, or frustrating, the natural tendency is to drop it and do something else. This substitute behavior is called **displacement activity.** Such displacement activity is a way of avoiding the task at hand, but it too can be controlled to the student's benefit. The chart on page 52 lists displacement activities that will actually reinforce your studying while allowing you to withdraw momentarily from your central task.

If you try these and similar strategies but still find your study thwarted by internal distractions, you may need to pose larger questions to yourself. Is your study schedule really in tune with your mental and biological rhythms? Is there some important unfinished business that your unconscious is trying to remind you to do? If so, the only effective strategy may be to take care of that business first.

Displacement Activities

Activity	Results
Browsing Leafing through the book one is reading, examining the table of contents, the index, the rest of the chapter, the pictures—looking at whatever suggests itself in a relaxed way.	Shift of perspective, like changing the lens of a camera from telescopic to wide angle. This enables the reader to relax and at the same time become familiar with the larger context of the book.
Drawing Making notes, maps, or diagrams to create a kind of status report on what you have learned thus far.	Provides a check on comprehension and indicates what the study process is yielding. An additional benefit is the product itself, which may be a study aid.
Planning Planning for the next break. This might involve deciding how far to go before stopping, deciding what to do, and planning how to get back to work.	A time management maneuver that puts a sensible limit on one's present effort and sets a reward for persevering.
Physical Movement Standing, pacing around the room while thinking about the task, doing forward bends to increase blood flow to the brain.	Physical activity that may stimulate thought processes. Because your body may become less active during periods of concentration, this may serve to speed up circulation and release tension collected in tightened muscles.
Changing Location Moving to another setting more conducive to studying.	Removing oneself from distractions such as conversation, food, and, for some, too much silence.
Breathing Breathing deeply according to any technique that involves rhythmic and slow-paced inhalation and exhalation.	Transports oxygen to the brain and eliminates toxins from the system. For many, has proven to be an effective and quick means of reducing tension.

If your inability to concentrate is becoming a common occurrence, with strong emotions crowding your mind, you may be getting a message that there are issues in your life you need to face. The sooner you do so, the sooner you will have access to all of your energy and the sooner you can devote it to your schoolwork and other activities. If the issues can't be resolved at this time, you may need to assign some space for them in your thoughts but reserve a substantial area for the tasks you can do. A journal may be helpful here as a place to maintain the necessary inner dialogue that accompanies pressing issues in life.

■

PERSONAL LEARNING QUESTIONS

**Does your schedule really reflect your basic priorities?
Does your schedule on a typical day take advantage of your
most alert periods? How effective have your study breaks been
over the past week? How might you change these patterns to
get maximum benefit from the time you devote to studying?**

■

Setting your books aside guilt-free for a while is a luxury you should enjoy. It is purchased by careful planning. If you postpone most of your studying until the night before a test, you are pressuring yourself, giving up options, and perhaps setting yourself up for disappointment that will affect your subsequent studying. On the other hand, if you carefully manage your time, you will be able to make shifts in your schedule and still have plenty of time to prepare.

Good time management is also a key to success in any career. All the ways of working with time presented in this chapter are strategies you can use in the workplace.

APPLICATION EXERCISES

1. Take an inventory of your reasons for being in college and the goals you want to accomplish. Make a list of long-term goals, including personal and career goals. Then make a list of immediate goals concerning what you want to get out of your college experience now. These should include both intellectual goals and social goals.

2. Relate your long- and short-term goals to your history course. How might your history course contribute to achieving these goals?

3. On a scale of 1 (poor) to 5 (excellent), rate yourself on each of the following:

   Nutrition
   Exercise
   Sleep
   Avoidance of destructive behavior

4. The best way to begin any time management program is to assess how you use your time now. A week is a good unit of time for this purpose. Do a "time and motion" study on yourself, keeping track in hour blocks of how you use your time. You don't need to be elaborate—just note the major activity for each hour. The following will help you organize your baseline data.

Hour	Monday	Tuesday	Wednesday	Thursday	Friday	Saturday	Sunday
6:00							
7:00							
8:00							
9:00							
10:00							
11:00							
12:00							
1:00							
2:00							
3:00							
4:00							
5:00							
6:00							
7:00							
8:00							
9:00							
10:00							
11:00							
12:00 + hours awake after mid-night							

5. Now, create a list of categories for the major activities in your life. These will no doubt include, but not be limited to, eating, sleeping, classes, studying, recreation, and socializing. If you have a job, that will also be a major category. You also need a housekeeping category for cleaning, doing laundry, and such tasks. If you have child care responsibilities, that will be an important category, too. Count the hours in your "baseline" week devoted to each activity and calculate its percentage of total hours in your schedule.

ACTIVITY	TOTAL HOURS	PERCENTAGE OF TIME
Eating		
Sleeping		
Classes		
Studying		
Recreation		
Socializing		
Job		
Housekeeping		

6. The first question to ask yourself is whether you are putting priority on items that are really important to you. If not, to what extent can you change how you use your time so that it contributes to your goals? After you have answered these questions, plan an "ideal" weekly schedule. Keep this ideal (and subsequent revisions of it) posted in a place where it will remind you of how you want to use your time.

Hour	Monday	Tuesday	Wednesday	Thursday	Friday	Saturday	Sunday
6:00							
7:00							
8:00							
9:00							
10:00							
11:00							
12:00							
1:00							
2:00							
3:00							
4:00							
5:00							
6:00							
7:00							
8:00							
9:00							
10:00							
11:00							
12:00 + hours awake after midnight							

TERMS TO KNOW

biorhythm patterns
displacement activity
learned helplessness
motivation
procrastination
three levels of planning
time management

CHAPTER 4

THINKING LIKE A HISTORIAN

GETTING • *How can you view history as a detective and*
FOCUSED *search for relevant clues?*

• *What does it mean to approach history the way that a judge approaches a decision in a trial?*

• *How can you decide which of several historical interpretations seems the most reasonable?*

• *How can you demonstrate that an interpretation is based on reasonable assumptions?*

• *How can the skills of a lawyer be useful to you in other life situations?*

THE HISTORIAN AS DETECTIVE

In Chapter 2, we suggested that you will have more success in your history courses if you learn to think like a historian. Then we described what kinds of topics contemporary historians think about. To do well in your history courses, however, you will also need to learn *how* historians think about these issues. Many students emerge from high school with ideas about how to do history that are very different than those of their college professors. Such students may work hard, but the return for their efforts will generally be limited.

Therefore, in this chapter we will suggest different ways of thinking about history that will help you get the most out of your work. First, we will argue that it may be useful to think of the historian as a kind of *detective*. Then, we will suggest that the historian often operates like a judge. Finally, we will compare the historian to a lawyer.

As you come to understand each of these metaphors, you will find it easier to understand what your instructor expects of you. You also will find that each hour you put into the course will produce greater rewards.

Learning to Forget

Dr. Watson was shocked to discover that Sherlock Holmes was not aware of the theory that the earth revolves around the sun. He was even more surprised to discover that the detective intended to forget this new information as soon as possible. Holmes knew that even his massive brain could not store all the facts in the modern world. Therefore, he was very careful to focus his attention on data that might be useful for his cases.

This story may be a bit extreme. However, it is worth remembering when you are faced with a standard history textbook. Think about how much information there is in the book. Pick it up and feel how heavy it is. Glance over a few pages. Now ask yourself: "Can I possibly memorize all this?" The answer, almost certainly, is "No." And, even if you could remember everything, how could you possibly sort through all these facts during a one-hour exam?

This, however, is *not* what you are expected to do. *History is not primarily a matter of memorization*. If professional historians tried to remember every fact they encountered in their research, they would be overwhelmed in a few days. Memorizing is not their job. They are not garbage collectors. They do not pick up every fact that happens to be lying around.

Instead, historians act like detectives. Like Sherlock Holmes, they decide what is important to remember and what can be safely forgotten. They carefully sift through the facts to discover the clues that are useful to them. The rest, they forget.

This is how you should approach learning in the great majority of history classes. You may occasionally find yourself in a history course in which you are expected to memorize random facts. In that situation, there is no alternative except to use your memory as best you can. It is more likely, however, that your instructors will expect you to approach the readings and lectures as a detective. Thus, your first task is to learn how to look for clues and how to ignore irrelevant information.

Let us see how this might be done in the case of a paragraph from a typical Western civilization textbook. These sentences are part of a section on "The Urban Landscape," which describes how cities in Europe changed in the late nineteenth century.

France led the way with other distinctive features of the modern city. Using wrought iron and steel, Parisian developers built large, glass-covered galleries in which independent shops and cafés were situated, and by the 1880s Moscow had followed the example. The first major department store was the Bon Marché in Paris. By buying in quantity, department stores could sell a wide range of mass-made goods inexpensively, thus making the products of industrial civilization available to workers and the lower middle class.[1]

This paragraph poses real problems if you think history is all memorization. There are at least five facts in the first two sentences alone.

1. In the late nineteenth century, France was ahead of other countries in developing the characteristics of the modern city.

2. Parisian developers used wrought iron and steel.

3. They built large glass-covered galleries.

4. Independent shops and cafés were placed in these galleries.

5. By 1880, the same thing was being done in Moscow.

When you multiply these facts by the thousands of sentences in the textbook, the job seems impossible. Keep in mind, though, that you are supposed to be a detective, not a garbage collector. You only have to remember the relevant facts.

---

[1]Richard L. Greaves, Robert Zaller, Philip V. Cannistraro, Rhoads Murphey, *Civilizations of the World,* Vol. II (New York: Harper and Row, 1990), p. 774.

Think of yourself as a detective trying to solve the mystery: "How did economic changes affect different social groups in the late nineteenth century." Much of the material in the sample paragraph then becomes irrelevant. It would not matter, for example, whether the Parisian galleries were made of wrought iron and steel or whether they were made out of spun sugar.

As a good detective, though, you will automatically stop when you read, "Department stores could sell a wide range of mass-made goods inexpensively, thus making the products of industrial civilization available to workers and the **lower middle class**." Here is an essential clue that will help you understand how different groups were affected by the Industrial Revolution. If, for example, you were asked on an exam to describe the impact of the Industrial Revolution, you could include the sentence: "The new department stores provided the workers and the lower middle class with cheap mass-produced goods."

There are other, lesser clues you might also want to collect—provided you have extra room in your mind. If, for example, you happened to remember that one of the early department stores was called "Bon Marché," you could use this fact. You might write, "New department stores, such as Bon Marché in Paris, provided the workers and the lower middle class with cheap, mass-produced goods." This would be more impressive to your teacher, but you probably could do fine without it.

■

Personal Learning Questions

How can you distinguish important clues from irrelevant details in studying history? Read over a paragraph from the readings assigned in your course for this week. Can you separate the important clues from the rest?

■

Knowing What to Remember

Identifying the Crucial Issues: Accepting a Case   The world is filled with potential clues, but each is useful only in solving a particular case. A detective cannot begin to evaluate these clues until he or she is trying to solve a particular case. The same is true when you work as a historian. You can begin to search for relevant clues only after you have set out to solve a particular mystery.

The classic detective had it easy. The doorbell rang at 221B Baker Street, and a prospective client was shown into Holmes's study. He or she told a story, made a request, and Holmes and Watson could began to work to solve the mystery. It is highly unlikely, however, that a stranger will come by your room and present you with a historical mystery. You will have to decide for yourself what "mysteries" are essential in your history course.

In some courses, you will be given considerable guidance in identifying the "cases" you must solve. As you move further along in history, however, the responsibility for identifying the important "cases" will fall more and more on you. This is particularly true if you write an original research paper or a senior thesis. Here, a large part of the task is to create a question that is worth answering.

It generally is useful to draw up a tentative list of important questions very early in the semester. The course syllabus and the textbook are good places to begin. They may be organized around big issues, each of which may provide the basis of a "case" for the historian/detective. The questions at the ends of sections may be particularly useful in this search.

As the semester progresses, lectures and/or discussions will help you refine your list of basic issues. What questions does your instructor seem to think need to be answered? What issues does he or she suggest need to be explained?

FIGURING OUT WHAT IS IMPORTANT IN YOUR HISTORY COURSE

1. Listen carefully to learn what is stressed in lectures.
2. Explore the syllabus. Examine subheadings and pay attention to how it is organized.
3. Look at the table of contents in the textbook, and see if there are study questions at the end of each chapter.
4. Look at exams used in the course in previous semesters.

In a survey of modern European history, for example, you might be faced with a great deal of evidence about what happened before, during, and after **World War I**. Before you can decide what parts of this information is worth remembering, you must define the most important "mysteries" concerning the war.

It is important to note that different courses may be organized around different issues. One course may devote a great deal of attention to the causes of the war. In that case, you would want to be on the lookout for clues relevant to the mystery of "Who Started the First World War?" In other courses, however, the focus might be on the impact of the war on different groups in society. Here, you might be watching for clues to help answer such questions as "How did the war affect the position of women in society?" In another course, attention might center on the impact of the war on European society in the postwar period. Here, the crucial question might be: "How did the war prepare the way for **fascism**?"

There will, of course, be more than one mystery to be solved in almost all history courses. In some courses that cover World War I, for example, it might be worth collecting clues to solve all three mysteries. In any case, the important thing is to formulate for yourself the important issues in the course. Then, you will have a basis for deciding what to remember and what to forget.

Identifying the Crucial Issues: A Case Study   Sandy felt overwhelmed by the details about the origins of classical Greek civilization in her Western civilization survey. Not only did she have to read several chapters in the textbook and some excerpts from writings by ancient Greeks, but she also had to attend a number of lectures on the subject, several of which included slide presentations.

Then, she remembered that she was supposed to act like a detective and not a garbage collector. She decided that her job was to separate out the relevant clues from this mass of details. First, Sandy had to have a clear sense of what mysteries she was trying to solve. She began by looking at the table of contents and subheadings in her textbook and the subdivisions on the syllabus. Then, she reviewed the lectures, paying particular attention to the outlines that her instructor had put on the board before class.

She saw immediately that this section of the course could be divided into two parts. The first covered the creation of Greek culture; the second covered its development and decline. Focusing on the first part, she soon realized that most of what was presented in the lectures and readings had something to do with one of three questions.

1. How did the mythology and heroic epics of early Greek culture shape the philosophy, art, and literature of classical Greece?

2. How did the Greek traditions find different expressions in Corinth, Sparta, and Athens?

3. To what extent was classical Greek civilization different than the earlier civilizations of the Middle East?

Now she had the three mysteries around which this part of the course was organized. As she read or reviewed her lectures, she could watch for clues that might help her solve these mysteries. This way, she had a basis for deciding what was worth remembering and what was not. And, she actually found that she could now remember a great deal more because the details fit into a larger pattern.

■

Personal Learning Questions

Do you have a clear sense of the mysteries facing you in the section of your history course you are currently studying? What are they?

■

Remembering What Is Important

Collecting Clues   Once you have identified the important mysteries to be solved, it is time to start collecting relevant clues. As you read, pick out those facts that help to answer the crucial questions. Use underlining and marginal notes to link this data to the questions you are trying to answer. Review the major "mysteries" prior to lectures and then listen for clues that may help you solve them. After class, go back over your notes and mark the material that might be relevant to each of the big questions of the course. Do not forget discussions. They provide an excellent opportunity to redefine your "cases" and to grasp what sorts of clues might help solve them.

As in any detective work, it is necessary from time to time to go back over the data to see if you have missed something. A reference in the lecture may make you recognize the relevance of something you discarded as unimportant in the previous day's readings. Similarly, another student's comment in discussion may help you see how you could use some information from the lectures to answer a potential essay question.

Finding Clues in Primary Documents The process of searching for relevant clues is particularly important when you have been assigned primary documents. You may be given a political essay, a legal document, a diary entry, or a piece of fiction to read. Inevitably, these will contain some irrelevant information. A novel, for example, will contain references to characters, random bits of dialogue, and elements of plot that have no connection to big questions in your course.

In the midst of these details, however, there will be crucial clues. Novels and other fictional works can convey a sense of how people interacted with each other in the past. Literature can provide clues about such topics as the experiences of different social classes or gender and race relations. These clues are useful, however, only if you are prepared to relate this material to the basic mysteries in the course.

Some Help from Chaucer Todd, a student in a freshman Western civilization course, was at first confused when the class was assigned to read "The Prologue" to Geoffrey Chaucer's *The Canterbury Tales*. Then, he remembered that in this section of the course one of the basic mysteries to be solved was: "How important was religion to the people of the Middle Ages?" With that issue in mind, he read the following description of a monk from the poem:

> A *Monk* there was, one of the finest sort
> Who rode the country; hunting was his sport,
> A manly man, to be an Abbot able;
> Many a dainty horse he had in stable. .   . .
> This Monk was therefore a good man to horse;
> Greyhounds he had, as swift as birds, of course.
> Hunting a hare or riding at a fence
> Was all his fun, he spared for no expense.[2]

Another student might have dismissed all this talk of horses and greyhounds as irrelevant to the course. Todd, however, was looking for clues to answer the question about religion. As a result, he recognized immediately that Chaucer was giving him information about how monks were viewed in the fourteenth century. On the next exam, Todd referred to this passage to support his argument that religion was not always as central to medieval life as it was supposed to be. This example demonstrated to the instructor that Todd knew how to make use of the reading, and it helped boost Todd's grade.

---

[2]Geoffrey Chaucer, *The Canterbury Tales*. (Baltimore, Maryland: Penguin Books, 1952), pp. 21–22.

Defining the central "mysteries" of the course also helped Todd in another way—it showed him what to forget. He remembered the irreligiousness of the monk because it was relevant to a central question. He quickly forgot that the character had greyhounds, though, because that piece of information did not help him solve his case.

Round up the Usual Suspects   At the end of a classic murder mystery, all the potential suspects typically are assembled and the clues are reconsidered. In preparing for an exam or even a class discussion, you will need to do much the same thing. You will need to reconsider each of the major questions raised by the course and assemble the relevant clues you have collected.

If you have operated like a detective from the beginning, this will be a piece of cake. You will have already tamed the flow of information coming in. You will have carefully separated the crucial clues from the mass of information around them. And, you will have connected each of these clues to a relevant question. You will be in charge, and you will be prepared to move to the next stage of the process: using the evidence to prove your case in "court."

THE HISTORIAN AS JUDGE

In some countries, people believe that guilt or innocence is obvious. The formalities of a trial therefore are considered unnecessary. All that matters is the collection of evidence to support the prosecutor's accusations. In our society, however, we believe that a judge or jury must listen to different interpretations of the facts before deciding which is most plausible. Even then, there is the possibility of an appeal or the introduction of new evidence.

Historians operate very much like judges in democratic societies. They do not believe that it is enough simply to collect data. They also must consider a number of different **interpretations** and decide which one is best supported by the evidence. And, their judgments are always open to appeal by later generations of historians.

Many students feel more comfortable with the role of historian-as-detective than that of historian-as-judge. They think that their job is finished when they have organized the facts. They wonder how they can be expected to make judgments about great historical questions when even the experts do not always agree.

In some history courses, students will, in fact, be able to stop with the collection of relevant data. They will be asked to remember the

DEALING WITH THE "DARK AGES"

George and Audrey are taking a course on medieval history. George assumes that historians have at their disposal certain absolute truths. He believes that his job is to memorize these truths and repeat them on exams. When his instructor discusses various ways of interpreting the Middle Ages, George just turns off his mind.

Audrey sees historians as judges who try to determine the most convincing explanation of the past. She tries to understand the different ways in which historians might view the period and what evidence or arguments might support each view.

At the end of the semester, both students are faced with the following exam question: "Some historians have viewed the early Middle Ages as a 'Dark Age' of economic, political, and cultural collapse. Others have seen it as a vital period in which the foundations of a new civilization were created. Provide arguments and evidence to support each position."

George is dismayed by the question. He panics, and randomly begins to throw facts down on paper. Audrey is prepared to present the evidence for both sides of the question and to explain why she picked one over the other. Guess which person does better on the exam.

basic facts and to repeat them on an exam. In other courses, however, students will be expected to behave like judges and to determine which interpretation of events is best supported by the facts. Students in such courses sometimes become confused. They are looking for the "right" answer, when instead they are given only competing interpretations of the evidence. Often they decide that their instructors or even historians in general are frauds, who cannot tell us anything meaningful about the past.

In this respect, however, historians are not different from judges. Both live in a world in which there are few absolute answers. Judges must always be prepared to reopen old cases when new evidence or new arguments surface. Similarly, any historical interpretation may someday be challenged.

This does not mean, however, that either the historian or the judge is "just making it up." Both go through a systematic process of weighing evidence. When they are finished, some explanations are judged to be more convincing than others.

Historians carefully consider various interpretations of the facts. They look at the evidence, analyze the arguments on all sides, and examine the **assumptions** that underlie these arguments. Then, they decide which interpretation seems most compatible with this evidence. It is this process that you will need to learn to achieve success in most history classrooms—and in most of the life situations you will face in the future.

The Responsibility and Pressure of Being a Judge

As a student of history, you will be expected to sift through evidence, to evaluate the validity of claims, to compare different interpretations, and finally to judge which interpretation you find most convincing. In some courses—most commonly introductory surveys—this aspect of history may not be explicit. The lectures and the readings may give you a single interpretation of the major issues in the course, and there may be little or no discussion of other interpretations.

Even here, though, it is important to remember that historians operate like judges. All the evidence presented in lectures and readings is there to allow one to make a judgment about the past. Moreover, history exams are filled with words such as "defend," "support," "provide examples of," and "explain." Such key words assume that history is a process of choosing among alternative explanations.

As you move along in history courses, you probably will be asked to play the role of judge more explicitly. You may be presented with multiple interpretations of the major issues. Lectures may present explanations that differ from those in some of the readings. Similarly, you may be asked to read essays by historians who interpret the past in different ways.

Asking students to play the role of judge is both a compliment and a challenge. In such classes, students are expected to carefully examine the arguments, to compare them with other material from the course or from their experience, and to judge which argument seems to be the most plausible. There are few exercises in a college career that are more useful for preparing to deal with life.

Being asked to choose among various possible interpretations may be a compliment, but it may also create anxiety. Students no longer have the security of a single interpretation that they can feed back to the instructor. They frequently ask themselves: "How am I supposed to know which explanation is the best?"

You will probably be less worried by such questions if you recognize that there is nothing unique about this process. It is what you do in everyday life. You are constantly interpreting situations around you, often on the basis of limited evidence. When, for example, you decide whether someone is lying or telling the truth, you probably consider several possible explanations of the relevant events to determine which seems most likely. Judging historical explanations is really no different.

Choosing an Interpretation

Once you are confident that you have assembled a strong body of evidence, it is wise to make a list of possible interpretations. Consider each of the major issues of the course, and see what explanations have been offered for each in the lectures and readings. See if you can come up with other possible interpretations.

Then, compare all the interpretations you have assembled for each major question. How convincing is each explanation? What evidence would seem to support it? What evidence makes it seem less valid? Do any of the explanations rest on unreasonable assumptions? Are they all logically consistent?

After you have thought about all this for a while, come to your own conclusions, just as you do in the thousand and one other interpretations you make each day. Decide which explanation is most convincing and why it is more plausible than its competitors.

The process of considering multiple interpretations does, of course, take time. You can easily do it when you are writing a paper or completing a take-home test. You may find it more difficult, however, in the midst of an in-class exam. Therefore, it is a good idea to begin thinking about the major explanations before you go into the exam room. Already have in mind what bits of evidence and what arguments are most relevant to each interpretation. The questions that appear on the exam may not focus specifically on the issues you have been thinking about, but you will find that you have already organized the material in your mind.

There remains a final question: what kinds of criteria do historians use in deciding which interpretation is most convincing. This is a rather subtle process, and it is difficult to provide a "cookbook" for historical interpretation. However, the ways historians make their judgments can be seen by looking at a particular case.

There are, for example, a number of different ways to explain the German defeat in World War I. Some historians would argue that Germany was simply fighting too many nations. Others would explain the defeat in terms of military strategy. Some would argue that the economic blockade of Germany slowly exhausted its ability to supply its troops. Still other historians would stress the entry of the United States into the war in 1917. Finally, in the 1920s, Hitler himself vehemently insisted that Germany collapsed because it was "stabbed in the back" by a Jewish-Socialist conspiracy.

If you were in a course in which all of these positions were presented, how would you go about deciding which arguments are most convincing? The first step would be to examine the evidence presented to support each argument. Does the evidence seem to be reliable? If so, does it really prove what it is supposed to prove?

Next, reexamine the evidence that has met these tests and determine whether it makes each explanation more or less convincing. Imagine, for example, that you are considering the argument that economic isolation caused the defeat of Germany. You may find evidence that German leaders took extreme measures to break the Allied economic blockade. This would give more weight to this interpretation of the defeat. By contrast, information about successful efforts by German scientists to find substitutes for materials they could not produce at home would weaken this argument.

Once you have weighed all the evidence in this manner, it is time to decide which explanation is most convincing. In many ways, this decision is less important than the process by which it is created. Your instructor may not agree with your judgment. Still, if you can demonstrate that you have carefully considered all the arguments supporting each explanation, you are apt to do quite well.

In the end, you will not have found the ultimate truth about the end of World War I. You may in the future change your own opinion about the matter as you receive new evidence. However, you will have narrowed the range of reasonable explanations and be in a much better position to reject certain interpretations as nonsense. If this seems insignificant, just consider how history might have been different if millions of Germans had undergone such a process and decided that Hitler's "stabbed-in-the-back" theory was hogwash.

■

PERSONAL LEARNING QUESTIONS

How have you dealt in the past with the responsibility and pressure of making judgments about particular situations? How will you deal with such responsibility and pressure in the future?

■

THE HISTORIAN AS LAWYER

We have now seen the historian in two major roles: the detective searching for relevant clues and the judge deciding which interpretation of the data is most convincing. Now it is time to add a third: the historian as lawyer, presenting a case to a jury.

To operate like a historian, you must be able to play all three roles. Like a detective, you will need to build a body of relevant evidence. Like a judge, you will need to consider and evaluate different interpretations. And, like a lawyer, you will need to present a convincing case that your interpretation is a credible one. Perfecting these skills is crucial for success in most history courses. More importantly, however, these skills will provide you with a model for dealing with countless situations you will face throughout your life.

Learning to Think Like a Lawyer

The idea of trying to think like a lawyer may seem a bit intimidating when you are still an undergraduate. Almost certainly, however, you already have a model for this process in your mind. Think back to the courtroom dramas you have seen on television or in the movies. There is almost always a dramatic scene in which the trial lawyer sums up his or her case to the jury. What exactly does a good lawyer do?

First, he or she presents an interpretation of the case. Second, the effective lawyer demonstrates that the evidence supports this interpretation. Third, the lawyer shows that his or her interpretation is based on a series of reasonable assumptions about how human beings work. And, finally, the lawyer considers other possible interpretations of the evidence and shows why they are less credible. A clever attorney may choose to alter the order of these elements, but presentations to a judge or jury will almost always contain all four.

Again, we should stress that these four operations will not all be needed in every history course. In some courses, memorization and straight detective work are central. However, the four basic skills of the

PRESENTING YOUR CASE

Like a trial lawyer, you will need to do four things to make a successful case in your history class.

- Present an *interpretation* of some historical phenomenon.
- Present *evidence* that supports this interpretation.
- Demonstrate that this interpretation rests on reasonable *assumptions*.
- Produce *refutations* of other possible interpretations, demonstrating that they are less credible.

lawyer *will* be needed in almost any course involving essay exams, discussions, or research papers and in many courses that have multiple choice exams.

Interpretation

A Particularly Inept Trial Lawyer   A hush falls over the courtroom as the defense lawyer in a murder trial looks at the jury and begins to sum up the case: "On the morning of May 15, my client got up at 7:00 A.M., ate breakfast, got dressed, and drove in on the freeway to work." One fact follows another for the next three hours, and then the attorney sits down without another word. It takes the jury only 15 minutes to convict the defendant.

Such a scenario is, of course, absurd. No competent trial lawyer is going to dump facts in the lap of a jury and assume that its members will draw the appropriate conclusions. Every year, however, thousands of undergraduates in history classes operate exactly like the inept lawyer in this story. Faced with an essay exam or a paper, they write down one fact after another as fast as they can. They assume that everything else will take care of itself.

They may have managed to separate out the relevant facts. The result, though, is apt to look more like a shopping list than a historical argument, and shopping lists do not generally get high grades in history courses.

Adding the "How" and the "Why"   To avoid such an experience, it is important to recognize what was missing in the courtroom summation

A TALE OF TWO STUDENTS
OR
HOW LAWYERS SCORE ON HISTORY EXAMS

To understand the importance of creating an interpretation, imagine two students faced with an essay exam on the causes of the American Civil War.

Student 1 reads the question and writes down everything he knows about the topic. He stuffs into the essay information about the history of slavery, abolitionism, the Missouri Compromise, the Dred Scott decision, and a dozen other items. After an hour, he leaves the exam feeling confident that the question has been answered. The grader, however, is left in the position of the jury listening to an inept defense attorney. There is a pile of evidence, but it has not been used to explain anything. The relevance and significance of the facts have not been made clear. All of this may add up to a convincing case in the student's mind, but the instructor can only grade what is on paper.

Student 2 begins the same exam by arguing that the presence of slavery in the South made the Civil War almost inevitable. She then presents the same evidence as the first student, but uses each fact to support her argument. At the end, she presents her interpretation a second time and sums up how the evidence proves her case.

The grader is impressed by this exam. The student clearly has an interpretation and offers evidence to support it. She obviously not only memorized facts, but is able to show how they fit together in a larger pattern. She has, in short, operated like a good trial lawyer, and she receives an A.

presented earlier. Trial lawyers are expected to explain not simply *that* something happened, but also *how* and, quite often, *why* it happened. The events have to be fit together into an intelligible story—or, to use a word quite popular among historians today, a "narrative." The motivations of the participants have to be explained. The meaning of the facts has to be made clear. An interpretation has to be created. Only then does the jury have something with which to work.

This is precisely what you need to do in your history course. Tell what happened and how it happened. Provide an interpretation or explanation of why it happened. And, organize everything into a case in which relevant evidence and rational arguments make your interpretation seem more credible than other ways of explaining the phenomenon.

■

PERSONAL LEARNING QUESTIONS

Think of an essay question from the past for which you received a low grade. How would approaching the question like a lawyer have helped you receive a better grade?

■

Evidence

Another Inept Trial Lawyer   Once again, a hush falls over the courtroom as the summation begins. The defense attorney rises and says: "My client is innocent. The crimes she is accused of committing were done by the butler. She should be set free and that's all there is to it." The lawyer sits down, and once again, the defendant is convicted almost immediately.

This attorney has moved to the opposite extreme from the one in our last example, and has presented an interpretation without evidence. This is a bad strategy to use in both the courtroom and the history classroom, but it is a trap into which many history students fall.

HOW TO ANSWER AN ESSAY QUESTION WITHOUT EVIDENCE (AND WITHOUT A GOOD GRADE)

Students taking an essay exam in a world history course were asked to support or attack the following statement: "Roman civilization depended entirely on the creativity of the Greeks." One student proceeded to write about how much she preferred the ancient Greeks to the Romans. She insisted that the Romans were culturally inferior, militaristic, and cruel. Although she had studied hard for the test, she received a C+. She returned to her dorm room and complained that the instructor was "biased."

Another student took the same position on this question. He, however, supported his position with specific evidence about Greek and Roman architecture, drama, philosophy, and political systems. The instructor happened to have a much higher opinion of Roman culture than either of these students. Nevertheless, she gave the second paper an A, because it demonstrated both an understanding of the facts and an ability to use them to defend a particular position.

When students realize that historians deal in interpretations, many of them jump to the conclusion that all historical explanations are just statements of personal preference. They do not see why evidence must be brought into the matter. When challenged, they are apt to respond that their opinions are as good as anyone else's. If they receive low grades, they generally complain that the instructor is trying to impose his or her views on the class.

What such students do not understand is that historians—like judges—must systematically weigh evidence before they can make decisions. There may be no absolute and final truth in either the history classroom or the courtroom. Some interpretations, however, are based on detailed knowledge and careful analysis of the historical situation. Others are wild guesses, created without any serious thought or study.

The carefully considered use of evidence can separate reasonable from unreasonable interpretations. It can convince your instructor that you are in a position to make a reasoned choice of interpretations. And, throughout your life, it can help you distinguish between reasonable explanations and absurd assertions.

Using Evidence in a Convincing Manner   There are two aspects to the successful use of evidence on exams or in discussions. First, you must be certain to find the most powerful pieces of evidence. This involves the detective work discussed earlier in this chapter, and generally results from careful review of the readings and the lecture notes. Second, you must clarify how each piece of evidence makes your interpretation the most credible one. Facts rarely, if ever, speak for themselves. It is necessary to demonstrate how each piece of evidence makes your interpretation believable.

You will have many opportunities to perfect this art. During discussions, you can practice presenting evidence to support your position and observe how well others do the same. And, when you are preparing for exams, you can make lists of bits of evidence that might be used to support various interpretations—just as lawyers do when preparing for trials.

.

PERSONAL LEARNING QUESTIONS
**Think of a recent example in which you tried to persuade others
to your point of view. Were you successful? If not, what
evidence could you have used to strengthen your position?**

.

Assumptions

Yet Another Incompetent Lawyer Let us consider yet another way that a defense attorney can fail his or her client. This time, the lawyer does present an interpretation of the events and does support this interpretation with relevant evidence. She insists that the defendant could not possibly have committed the murder because he is a man who loves animals. This interpretation is carefully supported by evidence that demonstrates that the defendant has many pets and treats them all well. When the jury begins deliberations, one member (an animal rights supporter) holds out for 10 minutes and then joins the majority in voting to convict. The defendant is sentenced to life in prison.

What is the problem this time? An interpretation was given and evidence was presented. However, the entire case rested on the assumption that people who like animals can not commit murder. The members of the jury did not find this to be a reasonable assumption, and thus they ignored the defense attorney's arguments.

THE PROCESS OF MAKING ASSUMPTIONS

EVIDENCE

1. French peasants were hungry.
2. The peasants revolted.

INTERPRETATION

French peasants revolted because they were hungry.

ASSUMPTION

Hunger can motivate people to revolt.

The Problem of Making Assumptions in History All arguments depend on certain assumptions about how the physical world, society, and human beings operate. There is nothing wrong with making assumptions. In fact, is impossible to say anything about human actions without making certain assumptions about how people operate.

All assumptions, however, are not the same. Some are appropriate, and some are not. It all depends on the context. Today, for example, it is reasonable to assume that when one sends an income tax check to the government, it will not be pocketed by a clerk. In many places around

MAKING INAPPROPRIATE ASSUMPTIONS

What the student wrote on the exam:

"The Roman government forced Christians to swear allegiance to the God-Emperor in order to bring them back to paganism."

What the student assumed:

Roman leaders made a clear distinction between religion and politics.

Why the instructor was not convinced:

For most of Roman society, the state religion was a part of politics. Loyalty to the official gods was a form of supporting government.

What the student wrote on the exam:

"French peasants supported Joan of Arc because she was defending France against the English."

What the student assumed:

These fifteenth century peasants had a clear sense of being French.

Why the instructor was not convinced:

The idea of being part of a nation is a modern one. Most peasants of this period would have thought of themselves as coming from a village or, at most, a region—not from France.

What the student wrote on the exam:

"John Kennedy won the Democratic nomination because his youth and charm helped him defeat his rivals in the primaries."

What the student assumed:

In 1960, most delegates to political conventions were chosen in state primary elections.

Why the instructor was not convinced:

In this period, most delegates to political conventions still were selected by state party leaders, not by primary elections.

the world 200 years ago, though, it was assumed that tax collectors would take a cut of what they received. As this example shows, historians must be particularly careful about context when making assumptions. What is true for our own time may not be true for an earlier period.

There are several different kinds of false assumptions that students can make about the past. Some false assumptions rest on practical issues, such as the availability of technology or the organization of society. A student might assume, for example, that the inhabitants of one region knew about events in a distant area. In reality, before the development of modern systems of communication and transportation, individuals often knew little about events even in their own countries.

Another false assumption centers on the political context of other periods. When, for example, students read about "citizens" in ancient Greece, they often assume that the term included everyone. In reality, though, women and slaves—the majority of the population—were excluded from Greek democracy.

Perhaps the easiest mistake to make is assuming that people in other periods thought as we do now. In contemporary America, for example, certain kinds of economic opportunity will encourage people to take risks and make investments. Modern economics rests on such assumptions. It would be dangerous, however, to assume that peasants living in the Middle Ages operated in the same fashion. Their traditions, their economic situations, and pressure from other peasants might discourage risk-taking. Thus, what is a valid assumption about our society may not be true of an earlier period.

Similarly, each individual in our society generally holds to a single religion. A person may be Catholic or Protestant or Jewish or Muslim or something else, but he or she typically holds to that faith no matter what the context. In traditional China, however, this was not the case. An individual might be a **Confucian** in one context, a **Taoist** in another situation, and a **Buddhist** in a third. In such a society, conflicts among religions took on a form very different from our own.

Checking Your Assumptions in History   As we have indicated, it is very important that your notions about political systems, governments, gender roles, economics, art, religion, and a host of other topics be applicable to the time period you are studying. In most history courses, you will receive a great deal of guidance in this area. You will find information in the lectures and readings that describe how people lived and thought in the past. If you simply focus on recording facts, though, you may miss this background information. You must go beyond the details and try to understand something about what it was like to live in other periods.

In the process, you may have to reexamine some of your assumptions about what human beings are "naturally" like. You will have to explore the possibility that in other periods people acted very different than they do today. You will need to ask yourself whether behavior that is "natural" today was "natural" in the past. At the same time, you will need to use your imagination and take a leap into another world. As you read the textbook or listen to lectures, you will need to put yourself in the place of individuals in other eras.

Try to imagine how different the world must have looked to the people you are studying. Try to reconstruct their mental universe—their *mentalité*, to use the French term popular among historians today. Then, reconsider your interpretations and evidence to be sure that your argument is really appropriate to the society you are studying.

Discussion can be particularly useful in learning which assumptions are reasonable. Here you can actively explore the world of the past and check out whether your ideas are valid. And, in the process, you can widen your ideas about what it means to be human.

This can be one of the most enjoyable and useful aspects of taking a history course. On the one hand, it is an invitation to dream, to travel in your mind to distant times and places. On the other hand, the process of putting yourself in the minds of other generations can open up enormous life opportunities for you. You can learn to see possibilities that would never have occurred to you otherwise. In addition, the process will help you understand those in your own society who think in ways different than you.

■

PERSONAL LEARNING QUESTIONS
Do you have any false assumptions that might be holding you back in your history course? What are they? How can you get rid of them?

■

Counterarguments

A Fourth Lawyer You Do Not Want Defending You   Let us make one last trip to the courtroom. This time, the defense attorney presents a coherent interpretation of events, supports it with relevant evidence, and bases the arguments on assumptions that seem reasonable to the jury. After a five-hour deliberation, though, the jury votes to convict anyway. Why?

In this trial, the attorney presented an effective case. The prosecutor, however, offered a different interpretation of the events. The defense lawyer failed to make counterarguments to the prosecutor's interpretation, and some members of the jury were convinced that the prosecutor was right. After a long argument, these jury members convinced the rest of the jury.

Considering Other Interpretations This is an important lesson to carry into your history classroom. To be a successful student of history, it is not enough to present your own interpretation, to offer supporting evidence, and to base your position on appropriate assumptions. You must also demonstrate that your interpretation is more valid than others.

Thus, part of your job as a history student is to see that there are several different ways of looking at the evidence. In some courses, you will actually be presented with several interpretations. In others, you will have to come up with alternate explanations yourself. In either case, though, you cannot fully defend your interpretation until you

---

USING COUNTERARGUMENTS

June was faced with this question on a history exam: "Some historians have argued that the Cold War was caused almost entirely by the aggressive actions of the Soviet Union after the Second World War. Others have insisted that the United States also contributed to hostilities. Defend the position that you think most accurately reflects the events of the late 1940s."

She was well prepared for the exam and presented the thesis: "American actions contributed greatly to the Cold War." She defended this interpretation with specific evidence. And, she was careful to avoid inappropriate assumptions about the period. Her instructor liked the answer and gave her a B+.

Jeanne took the same position and covered many of the same points as June. However, she also stopped to counter the arguments on the other side. She knew that some historians had argued that the Soviet occupation of Eastern Europe was clear proof that that nation was entirely responsible for hostilities with the United States. Therefore, she offered arguments and evidence to show that the situation was more complex. The instructor was even more impressed with her argument than with June's, and he gave her a solid A.

---

have considered competing theories. And, once in a while, you may even decide that you are riding the wrong horse and that it is time to change to an interpretation that is more convincing.

Showing the Weaknesses of Other Interpretations You have now considered several interpretations and decided which is most convincing. The next step is to demonstrate why the other interpretations are not as valid as yours.

The arguments against competing theories can take many forms. You can demonstrate that another interpretation is logically inconsistent. You can show that your explanation accounts for the evidence better than others. You can argue that other interpretations rest on invalid assumptions about how things worked in the past. Or, you can present some combination of these arguments.

FOUR WAYS TO DEMONSTRATE THAT A COMPETING INTERPRETATION IS NOT AS VALID AS YOURS

1. Show how the other interpretation is logically inconsistent.
2. Demonstrate that your interpretation explains the evidence better.
3. Show that the other interpretation rests on inappropriate assumptions.
4. Combine two or more of these approaches.

In many situations, you may not have time to present all of these counterarguments. Still, having gone through this process will strengthen your argument and help you better understand the issues in the course.

■

PERSONAL LEARNING QUESTIONS

Think of the person you know who is most usually successful in debates. What skills does this person bring to the debates? What would you change about yourself to become as successful in debates as this person? How could you use these skills in your history course?

■

The Skills of the Lawyer

The four skills that we have explored in this section are crucial for success in most history courses. If you know how to present an interpretation, support it with evidence, base it on reasonable assumptions, and make counterarguments, then you know what it means to think like a historian.

If you have learned these skills, you have gained more than a good grade in your current course. You have gained crucial skills that will be of use in future courses and, more important, in life itself. It is the mastery of these four skills that makes us rational beings. If you consistently exercise these skills, you will be putting all of your mental power into achieving your life goals.

APPLICATION EXERCISES

1. Identify one or two of the major "cases" (historical questions) presented in a particular week of the course you are taking. Define the "case" and make a list of what might be useful to know about the case in order to understand it.

2. Photocopy a chapter from your textbook or from your lecture notes. Then complete the following steps:

   A. Make a list of the basic "mysteries" that need to be solved in this section of the course. Assign a specific color marker or other visual code to each.

   B. Black out everything that you are reasonably certain it is *not* crucial to remember.

   C. Go back through the sentences you have not blacked out and indicate which mystery each might help solve. Leave untouched everything about which you are unsure.

   D. Go back over the material that is neither blacked out nor marked. How much of this do you really need to remember? How much of it can be blacked out? Does some of this material suggest new mysteries that you should be trying to solve?

E. Go back over the colored sections and imagine how you might use this information to answer a hypothetical true/false, matching, or essay question on this material.

3. Consider an event that occurred in the recent past and write down some of the ways it has been explained. List the evidence that might be used for each interpretation, and come to a judgment concerning which explanation is most convincing.

4. Pick a major issue discussed in your course for which there was only one explanation given. Consider what other ways the phenomena might be explained.

5. Think of one of the major issues in the history course you are taking. Find the interpretation of that issue that you find most convincing. Now, imagine that you were trying to convince a jury that this was the most plausible way to explain this phenomenon. Prepare your final speech for the jury.

6. Explain to a friend how historians operate as detectives, as judges, and as lawyers. (Give it a try. It can be argued that a person never truly understands anything until she or he has explained it to someone else.)

TERMS TO KNOW

assumptions
Confucianism
fascism
interpretations
lower middle class
Taoism
World War I

CHAPTER 5

READING STRATEGIES FOR LEARNING HISTORY

GETTING FOCUSED

- *What strategies and skills can you develop to cope with the large amount of reading required in a history course?*

- *Do you regard reading as an active or passive activity? What can your mind be actively doing while you read?*

- *What is the difference between reading analytically and reading to memorize?*

- *What are some techniques for interacting with your textbook and the information in it while you are studying?*

- *How should you relate your reading assignments and lectures to each other?*

The roots of the word *history* reach back through Anglo-Saxon to the ancient Greek term *histor*, which means "a wise and learned person," and even further back to the Sanskrit word for knowledge. In modern English, history is the cousin of *story*. The study of history therefore is the gathering of human wisdom through stories. The content of history is an evolving mosaic of the human experience. For the history student, this accumulation of stories translates into a lot of reading.

STRATEGIC READING

To handle the sheer number of pages likely to be assigned in a history course, you will need to practice strategic reading. Having a **strategy** for reading will be useful to you throughout your life as, in virtually any career, you are faced with quantities of information to read.

Basically, there are three kinds of reading you'll do in a history class: reading to keep up with assignments and lectures, reading to prepare for exams, and reading for writing papers (research). In this chapter, we will concentrate on reading strategies for assignments and lectures. Chapters 7 and 8 will discuss reading strategies connected with exams and paper writing.

Reading for Assignments and Lectures

Being strategic means being active, using your mind to select and organize meaning. To succeed in this active process, think of the textbook as a living thing, the product of another active mind or minds that are far away and perhaps from another era. Through the medium of writing, distance and time have been overcome.

Talk back. Stop your reading after each few paragraphs or pages and ask questions that will make the textbook respond to you. Then, in your mind, construct the answers, glancing back over the print you've covered. If you write down these answers, you'll end up with a useful and coherent set of notes.

Forget what speed-reading experts say. You're likely to get little out of your reading if you don't stop for these conversations. As you practice this approach, you should ask questions such as the following:

What is the main topic or issue here?

Does the textbook suggest a position or bias?

Does the topic remind me of anything else I know?

Do I understand this topic or issue well enough, or do I need to find out more?

What are the most important concepts or ideas in the passage?

■

Personal Learning Questions

How do you read? What kinds of questions do you ask yourself as you read? How can you organize the material for yourself as you read?

Understanding the Architecture of History

Historians think much like architects. They build structures out of concepts and facts. Reading only for the latter is like reducing a house to lumber and nails. Strategic reading means that you look at the architecture of the reading, first at the structure as a whole, and then at the materials from which it is made. Therefore, you might begin with the design of the textbook itself, to understand how it represents the writers' structuring of the content of history. A typical textbook, for example, will have an elaborate table of contents section that lays out its content informatively, in some combination of time periods and themes.

ANALYTICAL READING

The same structural principle applies to passages within the textbook. Usually, each passage contains main ideas, secondary concepts, and supporting details. These structural elements can be seen in the following example.

> THE BANK WAR Meanwhile, President Jackson had extended his national popularity by declaring "war" on the Second Bank of the United States (BUS). Jackson had long harbored a mistrust of banks in general, especially of Amos Kendall of the Kitchen Cabinet, and other key presidential advisers shared these sentiments. To understand their "hard money" position, it is important to realize that the national government issued no paper money like that in circulation. Payment for goods and services might be in gold or silver coin (specie) or, more likely, in paper notes issued by private commercial banks. The value of these paper currency fluctuated greatly. The hard-money Democrats realized that large commercial transactions could not be carried on with specie. But they

believed that the common people, including small businessmen as well as farmers and wage earners, should not be saddled with the risk of being cheated by a speculative currency. They also knew that a policy favoring the greater circulation of gold and silver coin, which seemed magically endowed with some fixed and "natural" value, would win votes for the party.[1]

From Details to Main Ideas

This paragraph may seem like a heap of details. There are at least four proper names, six terms for money, four references to groups or institutions, and three varieties of "common people." These are used to build complex concepts such as events and developments: the opposition of Democrats to BUS, the unreliability of speculative money, the impracticality of hard money, and the Democrats' strategies for gaining votes.

These complex concepts, in turn, are the elements of main ideas, the very broad concepts that summarize the entire passage. Not everyone, though, will agree on *the* main idea. This passage can be summarized in different ways. Here, for example, are two ways that it can be done.

The Democrats used the "speculative" versus "hard" money issue to attract popular support.

Lack of a national currency caused confusion in the money market and conflicts between government and the banking industry.

Notice that neither of these statements appears in the paragraph itself. Most of the time, you will have to compose your own main idea (summary) statement. This process of composing your own main idea is excellent for learning because you are translating book-meaning into knowledge of your own.

We can call this type of reading **analytical reading**. Such reading enables you to pick out the basic architecture of a passage: the main ideas or theses and the supporting details and concepts. If you practice analytical reading, your reading will parallel the architectural writing and thinking of the authors.

---

[1]Bernard Bailyn, Robert Dallek, David B. Davis, David H. Donald, John L. Thomas, and Gordon S. Wood, *The Great Republic: A History of the American People*, 3d ed. (Lexington, MA: D.C. Heath and Co., 1985), p. 376.

From Main Ideas to Details

To further clarify this process, let us look closely at one of our main ideas:

> *The Democrats used the "speculative" versus "hard" money issue to attract popular support.*

How is this main idea supported or clarified by specific details and concepts? The basic concepts of this statements are "The Democrats," "'speculative' versus 'hard' money," and "popular support." Each of these, in turn, is further explained in the paragraph. "The Democrats" discussed are Jackson, Van Buren, Benton, and Kendall. The issue of types of money is explained by what each type was and how it affected the economy. And, the words "small business as well as farmers and wage earners" identify who provided popular support. Thus we go from the highest level of generalization to concrete details.

This kind of organization facilitates remembering. If you have a good grasp of the main ideas, stated in your own words, you can go from these to more specific details. An excellent aid to analytical thinking is the acronym **IPSO**, or *Issue, Position, Support, Outcome.* Finding a main *issue* or question sets the topic. Finding the *position* or answer to an issue identifies the main idea. Finding the *support* for this idea selects the important details. And, finding the *outcome* provides a conclusion or reflective summary.

Having a pattern you can use is like having a good filing system. Details are filed in your mind under general categories, such as "Jackson Banking Policy." An effective organization help you find information you need for tests, especially essay questions.

QUESTIONS TO ASK YOURSELF AS YOU READ A PARAGRAPH

1. How can this paragraph be summarized in one sentence?
2. What are the basic elements of this sentence?
3. How is each of these elements explained or elaborated in the paragraph?
4. What is the main issue in the paragraph?
5. What position does the author take on this issue?
6. What kind of support does the author give for this position?
7. What outcome or conclusion does the author offer?

Applying the Concept of Analytical Reading

There is a vast difference between reading analytically and memorizing. Following is another paragraph from the history textbook excerpted earlier:

> *TOWARD A NATIONAL ECONOMY As the native Americans were pushed back, white settlers rushed in to occupy their lands. In 1860 the western frontier of settlement lay near the Missouri River, and between eastern Kansas and California there were hardly any white inhabitants except in the Mormon settlement in Utah and in the Spanish-speaking community at Santa Fe. Thirty years later, immigrants pushing west into the Great Plains and the Rocky Mountain region and pushing east from California formed a virtually uninterrupted pattern of settlement across the continent. In 1890 the superintendent of the United States census announced— a bit prematurely—that the frontier was gone. "Up to and including 1880 the country had a frontier settlement," he said, "but at present the unsettled area has been so broken into by isolated bodies of settlement that there can hardly be said to be a frontier line."[2]*

Let us imagine two students, Marcia and Anne, reading this passage. Marcia has a particularly good memory and generally relies on memorizing as a reading strategy. Anne, on the other hand, is more inclined to read analytically.

Marcia takes in the details of this passage, which include three dates, seven place names, four groups of people, and a number of complex concepts (such as displacement of Native Americans and the disappearance of the frontier). Faced with a question such as "Discuss the significance of the closing of the frontier for various groups of Americans in the last decades of the nineteenth century," Marcia just "flips through" the pages in her mind, finds the material she has memorized, and writes the following answer.

> *In 1860, the frontier was near the Missouri River. Between there and California there were few white settlements except for those in Utah and Santa Fe. Immigrants kept pushing west into the Great Plains and Rockies and east from California. In 1890, the head of the U.S. census said the frontier was closed. Perhaps this wasn't true, but more and more settlers were filling up the country.*

---

[2]Ibid., p. 523.

Unfortunately, this feat of memory does not answer the question. Marcia has not shown what these details have to do with the experiences of various groups of Americans. The question asks her to *do* something with the information, not just repeat it.

Anne has developed the habit of stopping at the end of passages and summarizing main ideas to herself or in the page margins. After reading our sample paragraph, she comes up with this main idea: "In the late 1800s, white settlers gradually displaced the Native American population and took over the continent." Having formulated this main idea, Anne pauses to relate it to other main ideas from her readings and lectures. This new idea then becomes part of a larger pattern she is developing about post-Civil War America. For example, she remembers a lecture on the contributions of African Americans and Asian Americans to westward expansion and notes that the passage refers only to "white settlers" and "white inhabitants." Her analytical reading is helping her to read critically.

Taking her cue from lectures, Anne decides that an important issue is expansion and the concept of the frontier. She wants to remember good supporting details for any general statement she makes. Because she uses her mind for reasoning rather than for memorizing, however, she knows she won't be able to remember every detail in the paragraph. She therefore is selective about what she thinks is important. The fact that in 1890 the superintendent of the census proclaimed the frontier closed seems important. The fact that "white" settlement ended in Kansas in 1860 does not.

When Anne reads the question "Discuss the significance of the closing of the frontier for various groups of Americans in the last decades of the nineteenth century," she turns to the "Post-Civil War America" file in her brain and retrieves the subfiles that may be of use. One, "Westward Expansion," comes to mind. She remembers both the position (in the late 1800s, white settlers gradually displaced the Native American population and took over the continent) and the supporting information (in 1890, the superintendent of the census proclaimed the frontier closed).

Anne, however, does not just use her memory. Rather, she links this material to the concepts and evidence filed in other subcategories (such as "The African American experience following the Civil War," "Immigration in the late nineteenth century," and "The development of labor unions after 1870." She draws connections between various ideas and information within the course, and she brings in information from outside.

In a matter of seconds she has a basic outline for her answer, drawn from both the textbook paragraph and other sources of knowledge. She then converts this outline into an opening paragraph that states a primary position.

> *When the superintendent of the U.S. census announced in 1890 that the frontier had disappeared, a major watershed had been crossed. The vast area of the West, which had been occupied primarily by Native Americans, was now covered in settlements of people descended from Europeans, Africans, and Asians.*

Having begun with a position supported by relevant facts, she now can discuss the impact of this change on four groups: Native Americans, white Americans, African Americans, and Asian Americans. Unlike Marcia, whose answer was over in the first paragraph, Anne has just begun a well organized and well argued essay.

Anne's paragraph contains fewer details than Marcia's. Anne, however, has linked two key ideas (the closing of the frontier and the displacement of Native Americans) and supported the linkage with selected details (one date, 1890, and an event, the announcement of the census bureau superintendent). What is important is that with this kind of beginning, she has set the tone for an effective discussion.

Is There Really Time for Analytical Reading?

The answer to this question is YES, *if* you've divided your reading into reasonable portions to be covered systematically throughout the course—a very important time management strategy for most students. Most course syllabi will provide each week's reading assignments in advance. Determine for yourself the following:

1. How many pages can I read at a sitting with full alertness and active processing?

2. How many pages are assigned this week?

3. Dividing the answer to question 1 into the answer to question 2, how many reading sessions do I need to plan in order to keep up with my reading this week and really understand the material?

One of the myths of reading is that it is a solitary process involving only the learner and the textbook. On the contrary, learning from reading can be a social process. Working together, students can speculate on the kinds of questions that might be asked on the next exam, discuss how they might answer them, and pool their relevant background knowledge. See Chapter 6 for more tips on conducting effective group learning.

Writing in the Textbook

Once you have gotten over any inhibitions learned in high school about writing in your textbooks, you may find text marking, which we'll call **annotating**, to be your most effective note-taking strategy. Keep in mind that annotating is not coloring! We have all seen pages so bright with highlighting that they are difficult to read. True annotating is itself an analytical process that exercises selection, judgment, and interpretation. Highlighting is usually employed sparingly, and in combination with other techniques such as underlining, circling, bracketing, and writing notes in margins.

One useful approach is to create categories of *kinds* of information and mark each in a unique way. For example, you might use one colored marker to indicate basic positions or interpretations taken in the material and use a marker of a contrasting color to indicate controversies where more than one interpretation is presented. You might underline basic supporting details (events, individuals, social groups, movements, places, and times) and bracket statements that provide causes and consequences. The categories, obviously, will depend on the nature of the material. Determining the categories as well as using them consistently will support your analytical reading.

■

PERSONAL LEARNING QUESTIONS

What kind of reading strategy do you currently use? Which elements of this strategy do you need to change in order to become a more analytical reader?

■

Talking to the Textbook

Use your pen to talk to the textbook. Here are some suggestions for such comments:[3]

1. Write brief summaries of the paragraphs in your own words.

2. List basic ideas (e.g., causes/effects; explanations; patterns of events).

---

[3]These suggestions are provided by Elizabeth Agnew, who has taught a learning skills course linked with a history course at Indiana University.

3. Note examples of concepts by writing "EX" in the margin.

4. Note puzzling or incomplete material with a "?" or by posing a question.

Now you are talking, too. After all, what is more boring than a monologue? You wouldn't spend much time talking to a person who wouldn't let you get a word in edgewise. Why let a textbook treat you that way?

Reader I

III. ISLAM

Origins of Islam

Sometime about ⑥⑩ in the Arabian town of Mecca, a merchant's son named Muhammad began to preach to the people, summoning them to repentance and reform. Generally, he brought his teachings together to form a new system of religious belief that he called Islam. The explosive impact of his preaching must be reckoned as one of the most extraordinary events of world history. Within a century after Muhammad's death his followers had conquered and partially converted territories larger than the old Roman Empire. Even today Islam remains the faith of more than 513 million people, about an eighth of the world's population.

Compare with Christianity and Judism?

ferment was no less pronounced. Several prophets, preaching new religious beliefs, had appeared in Arabia before Muhammad; and this indicates a growing dissatisfaction among the Arabs with their traditional paganism that gave no promise of an afterlife and offered no image of human destiny and the role of the Arabs in it. Both Christianity and Judaism had won numerous converts, but neither one was able to gain the adherence of the larger part of the people. The Arabs awaited a man who by the force of his vision could fuse these contending ideas–pagan, Christian, and Jewish–into a single, commanding, and authentic Arabian religion.

Islam's appeal within this political & environmental context

Questions: Nature of Arabic "Paganism"? Exact appeal of Muhammad teachings?

The Arabs

Arabian Pen.– physical characteristics

The Arabian Peninsula, the homeland of the Arabs, profoundly influenced their culture and history. Its vast interior and northern regions are dominated by steppes, wastelands, and some of the hottest and driest deserts of the world. The Arabs, however, had adapted to this harsh environment. They supported themselves by raising sheep and camels. These animals provided nearly all their necessities: meat, milk, wool and skins for clothes and tents, and fuel from dried camel dung. The Arabs were extremely proud of their family, race, language, skill, and way of life. The harsh environment and fierce pride made them spirited, tenacious, and formidable warriors.

The Arabian Peninsula was in a state of intense political and social ferment on the eve of Muhammad's appearance. The stronger political powers–the Persians, Byzantines, and Abyssinians across the Red Sea–tried repeatedly to subdue the Arabs, but they could not dominate them in their desert home. Religious

Relationship between environment and national character

Muhammad

Historians have little information that is certain about the founder of Islam. Muhammad was born at Mecca about 570 or 571. His father died before his birth, and his mother when he was six. After being raised by his uncle, Muhammad worked as a camel driver in mercantile caravans. He may have been illiterate and may have had no direct knowledge of the Jewish and Christian scriptures; but he did acquire a wide, if sometimes inaccurate, knowledge of the history and teaching of those two religions. About the age of twenty-five Muhammad married the widow of a rich merchant; thus freed from economic concerns, he gave himself to religious meditations in the desert outside Mecca.

In 610 the voice of the angel Gabriel spoke to Muhammad, and he continued to receive revelations in increasing frequency and length for the remainder of his life. After that event Muhammad began to preach publicly about personal moral reform, but only his wife and a small group of relatives initially accepted his

Story of Muhammad: Humble– uneducated background "Received" teachings from Gabriel Meditations

Reprinted by permission from Chambers, M., Grew, R., Herligh, D., Rabb, T., and Woloch, I. *The Western Experience*, 3rd ed. New York: Alfred Knopt, 1983.

There are limitations to annotating. One is the small amount of space available on a page for writing, so notes may be too abbreviated or difficult to read. Also, annotations are anchored to particular pages.

Reader II

228   The Early Medieval East CA. 300–1100

(margin note: Meccans didn't like his anti-paganism)

teachings. The Meccans feared him because his strictures against paganism seemed to threaten the position of Mecca as a center of pilgrimages. Mecca possessed a renowned shrine containing the Kaaba, a sacred black stone that was the object of pagan worship. Rejected in his native city, Muhammad accepted an invitation to come to Yathrib, a trading town 270 miles to the north, which he later renamed Medina.

(margin note: goes to Yathrib (Medina))

Muhammad's flight from Mecca to Yathrib is called the Hegira and occurred in 622; it later became the year 1 of the Islamic calendar. The Hegira was a turning point in Muhammad's career for two reasons: he became the political leader and governor of an important town, which gave him a base for the military expansion of the Islamic community; and his responsibilities as head of an independent town affected the character of his religious message. More and more it was concerned with public law, administration, and the practical problems of government.

(margin note: "Hegira"– 622)

Muhammad was more successful at Yathrib than he had been at Mecca in making converts. He told them that God ordered them to convert or conquer their neighbors; through enthusiastic proselytizing and war the community of believers grew rapidly. With this support Muhammad marched against the Meccans, defeating them at Badr in 624 and taking Mecca in 630. By his death in 632, Muhammad had given his religion a firm foundation on Arabian soil.

(margin note: ↑ converts)

(margin note: took Mecca 630, d. 632)

reader it imparts a powerful mood, one of uncompromising monotheism, of repeated and impassioned emphasis upon the unity, power, and presence of Allah. The mood is sustained by constant reiterations of set formulas praising Allah, his power, knowledge, mercy, justice, and concern for his people.

(margin note: disc. of Koran)

The chief obligation which Muhammad imposed upon his follwers was submission (the literal meaning of "Islam") to the will of Allah. Those who submit are Muslims, ("Muhammadan," which suggests that Muhammad claimed divinity, is an inappropriate usage.) Muhammad was little concerned with the subtleties of theology; he was interested in defining for Muslims the ethical and legal requirements for an upright life. Unlke Christianity, Islam retained this practical emphasis; jurisprudence, even more than speculative theology, remained the great intellectual interest of scholarship. Also in contrast to Christianity, Islam did not recognize a separate clergy and church, for there was no need for specialized intermediaries between Allah and his people. Allah was the direct ruler of the faithful on earth; he legislated for them in the Koran and administered through Muhammad, the Prophet, and his successors, the caliphs. Church and state were not separate entities, at least in theory. There was only the single, sacred community of Allah.

(margin note: Muslims people)

(margin note: disc. of Islam)

(margin note: no clergy)

The Religion of Islam

Instructed by the angel Gabriel, Muhammad passed on to his followers the words or prophecies of Allah (from *al ilāh,* "the God"). The collection of prophecies is known as the Koran; and Allah, in Islamic theology, is its true author. The Koran was written down in its present, official version from 651 to 652. The Koran often impresses the non-Muslim reader as chaotic and repetitious, but to the sympathetic

(margin note: Allah-God Koran-book)

Reprinted by permission from Chambers, M., Grew, R., Herligh, D., Rabb, T., and Woloch, I. *The Western Experience,* 3rd ed. New York: Alfred Knopt, 1983.

It is difficult to use them to connect material in different sections of the readings or to come up with broad ideas and interpretations. Separate notes give you more space and flexibility to develop your own thoughts.

■

PERSONAL LEARNING QUESTIONS

Have you captured the essence of each paragraph in your summaries? Did you get all the basic ideas in the text? Did you find some good examples that you could use in discussion or on an exam? Did you mark material that you did not understand fully so that you could be sure to study it more carefully before the next exam?

■

NOTE-CARD TECHNIQUES

Note cards provide major flexibility. By making a card for each "key concept" you identify, you will have a set of cards that you can organize into major categories. You can use these **key concept cards** to create maps and outlines of the material when studying for exams. A basic pattern for a 3 x 5 inch key concept card is shown below.

KEY CONCEPT (Word or phrase)   Page in text

Definition _____

Supporting details/examples_____

_____

_____

Linkages to other concepts _____

_____

_____

_____

The back of the card can be used for additional notes, such as drawing further connections between key concepts and other material. The following examples show the front and back sides of a key concept card on John Kennedy's presidency.

(FRONT)

PRESIDENT JOHN KENNEDY   *834–841*

JFK pres.: election '60, assassination '63. Seen as young, bright; also advisors;
appealed to American idealism: establishment of Peace Corps,
Alliance for Progress
Supported failed "counterinsurgency" operation to overthrow Castro
(Bay of Pigs), but also averted showdown w. Russian missiles
New Frontier: aims: help unemployment; increase middle-class housing;
increase minimum wage. Moderately successful.

(BACK)

Unger notes extreme political right hated JFK while the left criticized
him for being conservative, a "cold warrior."

Still questions concerning political factors in his death.

Oliver Stone's movie expression of widespread doubt.

The two examples on page 98 show a key concept card on the Gilded Age, with a key person on one side and a definition on the other.

Making note cards ensures active reading. To decide whether to make a card and what to put on it requires interaction with the textbook. The act of writing itself helps imprint that material in your memory.

Using the cards is even more helpful. Cards can be arranged to represent complex relationships among ideas in the textbook. You can use them to outline answers to potential essay questions. An excellent strategy is to think of a question like those asked in previous essay exams.

```
(FRONT)


GUSTAVUS SWIFT                              p. 465


  Entrepreneur successful through organizing meat-packing industry
effectively. Took advantage of advanced railroad system & invention of
refrigerated cars to centralize slaughtering & processing of cattle in
west before shipping to eastern cities.


  Between 1875–1890 number of cattle slaughtered jumped from
250,000 to 1 million (4x).
```

```
(BACK)


ENTREPRENEURSHIP
     Swift                    Carnegie                Note this theme
   organized               analyzed & cut             as organizing
  meat-packing         costs in steel industry    topic for this section


     Edison                  J.P. Morgan                  EXAM
  new technology      $$ invested. > industry          QUESTION**
  city-wide lighting   restored public confidence.
```

Then, select cards that pertain to this question. Spread the cards out on a table in various arrangements until you have created a model for your answer.

For example, if you imagine an exam question about the economy of post-Civil War America, cards on the Gilded Age would be useful. If you imagine a question asking you to compare the role of the federal government and the private sector in the economy at different times, cards on Kennedy and the Gilded Age could be used.

MAKING MAPS

Key concept cards can also be used to make maps of the material you are covering. Think about the function of a map, especially one that you might draw for someone going to a new place. It provides the essential information for reaching a particular goal. The same is true for reading maps. They show how concepts are related to each other in complex patterns. (See illustration on page 100.)

Here are guidelines to help you get started making maps if this is a new strategy for you:[4]

1. A map is your way of picturing the important *meaning* of a textbook. You can and should be creative.

2. Graphic representations can take many forms: flowcharts, branding trees, pie diagrams, fish bone maps (like the one pictured on page 100), matrices, charts—whatever suits you and the information. (See also illustrations on pages 101–102.)

3. To decide how to draw the map, survey the textbook to see the author's structure. You don't have to use this, but it will help, especially when you are a beginning mapper. There is nothing wrong with simplicity. A simple map representing the author's structure of the textbook can be enormously helpful.

4. As you become more experienced at making maps, you will probably move beyond the author's structure. You will use maps to create your own ideas about the meaning of a textbook. The three maps on pages 103–105 show quite different ways of organizing the same material.

What differences do you notice among the maps on pages 103–105? The first map is different from the other two in that it is a simpler map. All the items are in the same kind of balloons, connected by simple lines. Although it shows some connections among items, it is still much like a list.

The next two maps are organized around central questions, which makes them more complex. The second map addresses the question

---

[4]The guidelines provided here are adapted from Beau Fly Jones, Jean Pierce, and Barbara Hunter, "Teaching Students to Construct Graphic Representations," *Educational Leadership*, published by the Association by Curriculum and Development, (December 1988/January 1989), pp. 145–153.

INDUSTRIALISM (1865-1908) in the Gilded Age

CAUSES

T. Edison developed new technology; adapted electricity for home use to replace kerosene. Developed a business.

G. Swift organized meat-packing industry by using refrigerator rail cars and shipping meat East 1875-1900 Chicago slaughtering 4X

Jay Gould 1865-1908 a 7X increase in railroads transcontinental RR efficiency allowed for overnight travel, more safety, new markets for shipping. Gould and partners "watered the stock" of Erie RR, cheating Vanderbilt out of big $.

"CAPTAINS of INDUSTRY"
(entrepreneurs) organized, managed & assumed risks of business

A. Carnegie costcutter in RRs, iron, and steel; lowered price of steel–advanced engineering. "civic minded"

J. P. Morgan banker who oversaw mergers of several banks and helped pool $ for investment; helped restore Ams. trust in stocks following the 1873 panic

"SPOILERS" (financial manipulators)

"Work ethic" American values dating to Puritans emphasized hard work, thrift, honesty, etc. Horatio Alger novels show theme

J. Rockefeller Standard Oil Company formed a monopoly to avoid cutthroat competition— Rockefeller squeezed cheap shipping rates from RRs. By 1880 controls 92% of crude oil. Rockefeller's "trust" was illegal, so he formed a "holding company."

INTELLECTUAL FOUNDATION

Landgrants to individuals, colleges and RRs Morrill Land Grants, Pacific RR Acts

Regressive taxes

Protective Tariff

"Hand Off" policy of courts used 14th amendment to protect corporations from state and federal regulation –little concern for social justice

Defenders of Inequality

Ministers said it was a sign of God's approval

Philosophy of Adam Smith called for unrestricted pursuit of economic gain— "invisible hand" would spread benefits to all (laissez-faire)

Philosophy of Charles Darwin biological evolution applied to society—"Survival of the fittest" meant rich were fit to survive

EFFECTS

LIVING & WORKING CONDITIONS

Wages and life expectancies increase, but quality of life low

60 hour work week

Speed up or lose job to a machine

Health hazards (accidents)

Unemployment

Sum: despite poor living conditions, strikes and protests, most Americans kept "faith" in the system and rejected radical solutions (like socialism) meanwhile the country grew rapidly (economically)

SOCIAL MOBILITY AND PAY

"Labor Aristocrats"

Best for native white male laborers—could advance from unskilled to skilled jobs

Pay in 1880 from $1.30 to $2.45/day

Women earned only $1-2/ week in garment industry (many left to marry)

Black and immigrants also had low wages

WORKING CLASS PROTEST

TRADE UNIONS

1866 National Labor Union

1869 Knights of Labor By 1887 730,000 members— Knights demand 8 hr day $2 daily wage in Chicago in 1886— police attack anarchist bomb, K of L dies out

1886 American Fed. of Labor Skilled women only Avoided direct action (unsafe) By 1914 2 million members

SOCIALIST ALTERNATIVE

Marxists believed in overthrow by workers 1897 Debs found Socialist Party of America in 1912 Debs won 6% of presidential vote

PROTESTS

1876 Molly Maguires trial for murder of coal mine mgrs

1877 Nationwide RR Strike

1886 Haymarket Riot

1893 Homestead Strike at Carnegie Steel Mill

1894 Pullman (train) strike in Chicago (Debs led Strikers— later found Socialist Party

Network Tree

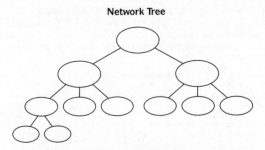

Used to show causal information (causes of poverty), a hierarchy (types of insects), or branching procedures (the circulatory system). Key frame questions: What is the superordinate category? What are the subordinate categories? How are they related? How many levels are there?

Fishbone Map

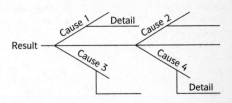

Used to show the causal interaction of a complex event (an election, a nuclear explosion) or complex phenomenon (juvenile delinquency, learning disabilities). Key frame questions: What are the factors that cause X? How do they interrelate? Are the factors that cause X the same as those that cause X to persist?

Human Interaction Outline

Goals	Goals
Person 1	Person 2
Group 1	Group 2

Interaction

Action ——————————▶ Reaction	
Action ◀—————— ——▶ Reaction 1 ——▶ Reaction 2	

Outcomes	Outcomes
Person 1	Person 2
Group 1	Group 2

Used to show the nature of an interaction between persons or groups (European settlers and American Indians). Key frame questions: Who are the persons or groups? What are their goals? Did they conflict or coorperate? What was the outcome for each person or group?

Cycle

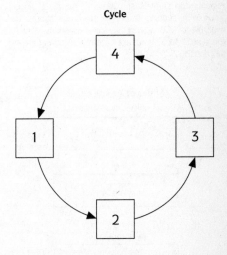

Used to show how a series of events interact to produce a set of results again (weather phenomena, cycles of achievement and failure, the life cycle). Key frame questions: What are the critical events in the cycle? How are they related? In what ways are they self-reinforcing?

From "Teaching Students to Construct Graphic Representations," by Beau Fly Jones, Jean Pierce, and Barbara Hunter, in *Educational Leadership,* December 1988/January 1989, pp. 145–153.

Graphic representations are visual illustrations of verbal statements. Frames are sets of questions or categories that are fundamental to understanding a given topic. Here are shown nine "generic" graphic forms with their corresponding frames. Also given are examples of topics that could be represented by each graphic forms. These graphics show at a glance the key parts of the whole and their relations, helping the learner to comprehend text and solve problems.

Spider Map

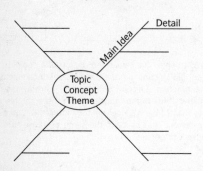

Used to describe the central idea: a thing (a geographic region), process (meiosis), concept (altruism), or proposition with support (experimental drugs should be available to AIDS victims). Key frame questions: What is the central idea? What are its attributes? What are its functions?

Series of Events Chain

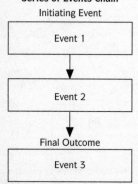

Used to describe the stages of something (the life cycle of a primate); the steps in a linear procedure (how to neutralize an acid); a sequence of events (how feudalism led to the formation of nation states); or the goals, actions, and outcomes of a historical figure or character in a novel (the rise and fall of Napoleon). Key frame questions: What is the object, procedure, or initiating event? What are the stages or steps? How do they lead to one another? What is the final outcome?

Continuum/Scale

Low	High

Used for time lines for showing historical events or ages (grade levels in school), degrees of something (weight), shades of meaning (Likert scales), or ratings scales (achievement in school). Key frame questions: What is being scaled? What are the end points?

Compare/Contrast Matrix

	Name 1	Name 2
Attribute 1		
Attribute 2		
Attribute 3		

Used to show similarities and differences between two things (people, places, events, ideas, ideas, etc.), Key frame questions: What things are being compared? How are they similar? How are they different?

Problem/Solution Outline

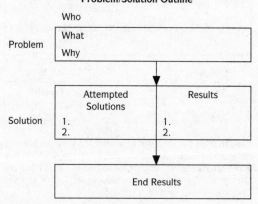

Used to represent a problem, attempted solutions, and results (the national debt). Key frame questions: What was the problem? Who had the problem? Why was it a problem? What attempts were made to solve the problem? Did those attempts succeed?

From "Teaching Students to Construct Graphic Representations," by Beau Fly Jones, Jean Pierce, and Barbara Hunter, in *Educational Leadership,* December 1988/January 1989, pp. 145–153.

A Network Tree

"Why come to the new world?" It uses a multidirectional flowchart, and it provides major categories of people who came to the new world, with details branching off from each major category. The third map begins with a more complex question, "How did the old world culture change?" This map uses essentially the same strategy of first categorizing main changes and then detailing each, but with more graphic differentiation through the use of boxes and arrows.

A group of students working together can create interesting maps. Designing and negotiating maps will facilitate a study session. This process can help students focus on the material, think together, and use their collective minds to greatest advantage.

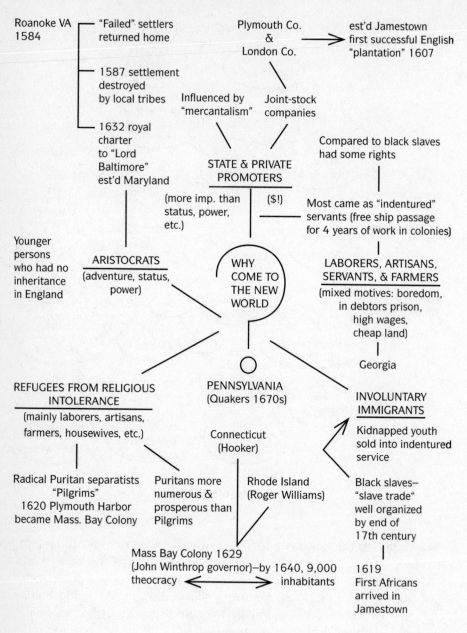

Roanoke VA 1584 — "Failed" settlers returned home

1587 settlement destroyed by local tribes

1632 royal charter to "Lord Baltimore" est'd Maryland

Plymouth Co. & London Co. → est'd Jamestown first successful English "plantation" 1607

Influenced by "mercantalism"   Joint-stock companies

STATE & PRIVATE PROMOTERS

Compared to black slaves had some rights

(more imp. than status, power, etc.)   ($!)   Most came as "indentured" servants (free ship passage for 4 years of work in colonies)

Younger persons who had no inheritance in England   ARISTOCRATS (adventure, status, power)

WHY COME TO THE NEW WORLD

LABORERS, ARTISANS, SERVANTS, & FARMERS (mixed motives: boredom, in debtors prison, high wages, cheap land)

Georgia

REFUGEES FROM RELIGIOUS INTOLERANCE (mainly laborers, artisans, farmers, housewives, etc.)

PENNSYLVANIA (Quakers 1670s)

INVOLUNTARY IMMIGRANTS

Kidnapped youth sold into indentured service

Connecticut (Hooker)

Radical Puritan separatists "Pilgrims" 1620 Plymouth Harbor became Mass. Bay Colony

Puritans more numerous & prosperous than Pilgrims

Rhode Island (Roger Williams)

Black slaves– "slave trade" well organized by end of 17th century

Mass Bay Colony 1629 (John Winthrop governor)–by 1640, 9,000 theocracy ⟺ inhabitants

1619 First Africans arrived in Jamestown

A Spider Map

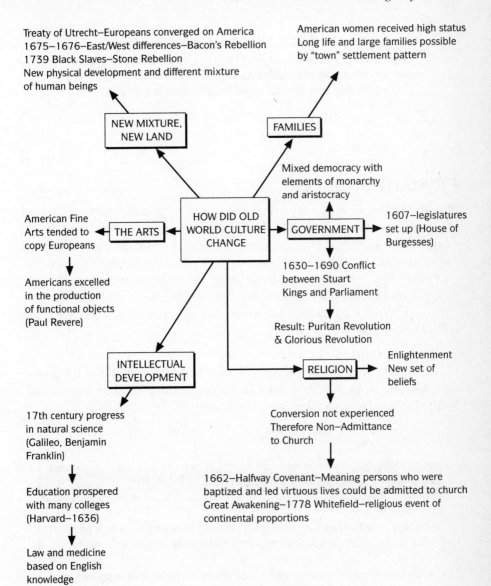

Treaty of Utrecht–Europeans converged on America
1675–1676–East/West differences–Bacon's Rebellion
1739 Black Slaves–Stone Rebellion
New physical development and different mixture
of human beings

NEW MIXTURE,
NEW LAND

FAMILIES

American women received high status
Long life and large families possible
by "town" settlement pattern

HOW DID OLD
WORLD CULTURE
CHANGE

Mixed democracy with
elements of monarchy
and aristocracy

THE ARTS

American Fine
Arts tended to
copy Europeans

Americans excelled
in the production
of functional objects
(Paul Revere)

GOVERNMENT

1607–legislatures
set up (House of
Burgesses)

1630–1690 Conflict
between Stuart
Kings and Parliament

Result: Puritan Revolution
& Glorious Revolution

INTELLECTUAL
DEVELOPMENT

17th century progress
in natural science
(Galileo, Benjamin
Franklin)

Education prospered
with many colleges
(Harvard–1636)

Law and medicine
based on English
knowledge

RELIGION

Enlightenment
New set of
beliefs

Conversion not experienced
Therefore Non–Admittance
to Church

1662–Halfway Covenant–Meaning persons who were
baptized and led virtuous lives could be admitted to church
Great Awakening–1778 Whitefield–religious event of
continental proportions

A Spider Map

■

PERSONAL LEARNING QUESTIONS

Which sort of map would best help you learn material in your history class that presently has you perplexed? Why would you find this sort of map more helpful than the others?

■

PRIMARY SOURCES

Not all reading is in history textbooks. Novels, poems, memoirs, travel accounts, essays, and political or religious tracts also may play an important role in some history courses. Private documents such as diaries or letters may be assigned. You also may encounter public documents such as wills, sermons, church or court records, or statistical reports. Original documents written during the period you are studying are called **primary sources**. Accounts *based* on these documents are called **secondary** sources.

Primary sources often are vivid and easy to remember. However, they also offer special challenges. They are like the material the historian uses to write the textbook. Therefore, to use primary sources effectively, you have to think like a historian.

USING PRIMARY SOURCES

A good way to begin to deal with primary sources is to ask why your instructor included them. Here are some possible reasons.

- **Primary sources can reinforce themes from the lectures and textbook.** Like slides or films, they are a means for conveying the basic concepts of the course. Reading an excerpt from *Oliver Twist* supplements a more abstract account of the Industrial Revolution as it may appear in a textbook.

- **They can provide a direct experience of the period.** Lines from a diary or sermon can put you in direct contact with the people who actually lived in the past. You can experience their language, their emotions, and their blind spots for yourself.

- **They help you compare your time period to the one you are studying.** No lecture can convey how much has changed over time as effectively as a seventeenth-century description of the toilette rituals of Louis XIV or the memoirs of an escaped slave.

- **They help you understand the perspectives among various groups in a given period.** The writings during the French Revolution by the English conservative Burke and the radical French leader Robespierre give you two strongly opposing viewpoints. Comparing European colonizers' accounts with those of the Asian or African people they colonized provide two contrasting views of imperialism.

- **Reading primary source documents helps you think like a historian.** If you ever thought that history consists of "a bunch of facts," primary sources will change your mind. All history rests on hypotheses, data of various kinds, interpretations, and arguments. Intelligent people can and do disagree on their interpretations of the past.

Relating Primary Material to Secondary Material

Before you begin reading a primary source document, think about the important issues in your course. For example, you may be studying the Civil War and be assigned private letters and memoirs that exemplify individuals' experiences in Shiloh. Perhaps an important theme of the course is the effects of the war on ordinary citizens. The documents of residents and common soldiers involved in battles would have a particular significance in understanding this aspect of war. On the other hand, if the theme of battle strategies is emphasized, you might read these documents differently.

Determining the Nature of the Document

Think about where, why, and by whom a document was written, who might have read it, and who might have agreed or disagreed with it. Such questions allow you to read the document actively and find ways to relate it to the larger themes of the course.

Some documents are primarily factual (though they can be viewed critically). Parish records of births and deaths, for example, would provide information about a given town at a given time. At the other extreme are documents that give one individual's very personal perspective. For example, a section from Hitler's *Mein Kampf* would not be assigned to convey factual information about the German defeat in World War I. However, reading this section would help you understand how Hitler viewed events of the 1910s and 1920s and appealed to the anger and fear of his contemporaries.

Usually, primary source materials must be read critically. For example, you may be assigned a novel by Jane Austin, representing nineteenth-century English society, or the memoirs of a Boer farmer in South Africa in the 1950s. You should begin by asking how the life situation and values of the writer might have shaped his or her account of contemporary life. You also can "read between the lines" and ask what the writer is omitting that may be important to understanding life in those times. As you identify possible distortions or biases, you will be understanding the perspective of a particular individual or group. At the same time, you will find accurate descriptions of life during that period. The same work can inform you both about the period generally and about how particular writers of the time interpreted it. Distinguishing between the two may be challenging, but it puts you in the shoes of a historian.

■

PERSONAL LEARNING QUESTIONS
**How does the primary source material assigned in your
history course relate to the textbook and the lectures? What
can you learn from the primary sources that is not fully
available in the textbook?**

■

WHEN TO READ? BEFORE OR AFTER THE LECTURE?

Most often, students are advised by their instructor to read the textbook before they attend the lecture. However, there are times when the opposite strategy works better. Let us consider the advantages of each.

Read First, Listen Later

This is the strategy-of-choice in a course where the lecture is tied closely to the textbook. Often, the lecturer assumes that students have read the textbook and he or she uses it as a basis for the lecture. It is also a good strategy to use when the lecture is rapid, covers a lot of material, or is not particularly well organized. Also, reading before the lecture will help you ask good questions in class.

To take full advantage of the read-first strategy, you may want to develop a note-taking system in which your reading notes organize your lecture notes. Use the careful structuring of most textbooks for this purpose. You may try a split-page strategy, with about one-third of the page for reading notes and two-thirds for lecture notes. A 50–50 split might also work, but leaving yourself more room for lecture notes will give you greater leeway to skip around and use the organization the reading notes provide. The following is an example of a split-page strategy used by a student who read the textbook material before attending the lecture. The arrows are the writer's short hand for "led to."

Reading Notes	Lecture Notes
THE TRUMAN PRESIDENCY FD Roosevelt died 4/45	Public call → return to normalcy

Last Years of New Deal:
  War growth of bureaucracy: 4X since '35
  No clear peacetime plan	

Military demobilization	ROLE OF ATOMIC BOMB

Labor discontent
  Taft-Hartley
  High inflation
	Growth of tensions during war & post-war settlement
	
	Poland's future improvement → Truman's election hopes

Beginning of COLD WAR	

Disputes over Germany & East. Europe
  Yalta agreement
  E-W Germany split
	Uncertainty re. significance of Yalta accords
	Different interpretations of E-W split

IRON CURTAIN	Fall of Czechoslovakia: last straw
US aid to Russia cut Soviet tightening of control over E. bloc	

Listen First, Read Later

This strategy may work better when the lecture is well organized and straightforward but the reading is difficult and complex. There may be numerous reading assignments of different kinds. The sheer amount of reading may require students to make decisions about what is more important and what is less important. The lecture can then provide a framework for planning one's reading strategy.

The following example shows how a student used the "listen first" strategy. By using this strategy, the student was able to organize priorities for extensive reading assignments drawn from both a regular textbook and a reader of chapters and articles.

Lecture Notes	Reading Notes
2/6/92 INDUSTRIAL REVOLUTION	See chapters 7 & 9 for examples and details

Enormity of change
Changes in production
   Smith's pin factory
     Impact division of labor
	pp. 676–682 New Shape of Industry
	Except fm. Wealth of Nations in reader

Changes in Consumption
  " " Society
  "   across time & geography
	Article on middle class life
	
	Change from agrarian society--find
	  references throughout texts

PROBLEM OF INTERPRETATION
  complexity of event--
  Different perspectives=dif. interpretations
	Compare reader articles from
	  Hard Times & Wealth of Nations

Example historical judgment	Different views on "Age of Progress" Text-Chapter. 25

Problems with traditional interpretations--
  Lack of representation of significant part
    of population
	Reader: Analysis of 3 contrasting views
	  of industrial revolution

Prevailing values reflect power structure	

Read-Listen-Read

Your best bet, of course, is to read before *and* after the lecture. This way, reading and listening have maximum impact on each other. To combine reading notes and lecture notes, you can use a three-part division of the page, with the center column being about the width of the other two combined. Write your initial reading notes on the left, your lecture notes in the center, and notes for further linkages on the right. The following example shows how this type of organization should look.

Reading Notes	Lecture Notes	More
		Include further reading references
Additional Lecture Notes	Additional Lecture Notes	Additional Lecture Notes

APPLICATION EXERCISES

1. For your next reading assignment, try an experiment. Choose three sections from the assignment, each of which should be about three to five pages in length.

   A. For the first section, copy the pages and annotate the text-book (or mark directly in your book) in a way that analyzes the structure of the information.

   B. For the second section, make a set of at least six key concept cards.

   C. For the third section, format a page according to one of the three formats discussed in the chapter and take separate reading notes that you will relate to the relevant lecture material.

   Which of these three strategies seemed most appropriate to your style and to the class material? Would a combination of strategies serve better than choosing just one? Can you devise your own versions of these and other strategies?

2. Now, select a comparable section and experiment with graphic mapping. How did mapping the material affect your thinking about it? Was this strategy more or less effective for you than conventional marking and note taking?

3. Consider the following questions, preferably in discussion with others.
   A. How does each strategy support or not support analytical reading?
   B. When does text marking seem the most appropriate strategy?
   C. When does making key concept cards seem the most appropriate strategy?
   D. When does making separate reading notes seem the most appropriate strategy?
   E. When does mapping seem the most appropriate strategy?

4. Devise your own "Personal Read-Study System" from the chapter strategies and others you adapt, design, or find in other sources.

TERMS TO KNOW

analytical reading
annotating
IPSO
key concept card
primary sources
secondary sources
strategy

CHAPTER 6

STUDY STRATEGIES FOR LEARNING HISTORY

GETTING FOCUSED

- *Do you learn best by seeing or hearing? If you are a "good listener," how can you make use of this skill in your history class?*

- *Can you listen effectively and takes notes at the same time?*

- *What should you do with your notes once you have taken them?*

- *How can talking about material help you understand and learn it better?*

- *How can you become an effective participant in class discussions?*

- *How can you organize and maintain a productive study group?*

LEARNING FROM LECTURES

Listening is an important process when you have to focus on someone lecturing for a full class period. A great deal of important material may be crammed into that lecture. How can you follow and comprehend everything while taking notes?

First, consider how well you control your attention during lectures. Are you spellbound the entire hour? Interested but occasionally find that your mind wanders? Do you tune in and out? Daydream most of the time? Must you fight for consciousness?

Attention control begins with your preparation before class. Your course syllabus lists reading assignments according to the dates of the class meetings. The lecture will often build on your knowledge of the readings. While doing the assigned reading, try to get a sense of how the lecture topic fits into the scheme of the overall course.

In addition to being in the proper frame of mind, make sure you're physically ready to concentrate. Get enough sleep so that you can remain alert during the lecture. Don't let a growling stomach or a sugar rush compete with the speaker.

Arrive at class early enough to get adjusted. Find your favorite seat, open your notebook, and make the mental transition from other thoughts to focusing on the lecture. You want to be ready for the crucial introduction, which generally gives an overview of the themes to be covered. If the instructor has put an outline on the chalkboard or on an overhead projector, copy it down before the lecturer begins speaking. Avoid spending a chunk of lecture time trying to catch up, because this can leave you confused for the remainder of the class session.

During the lecture, concentrate on paying attention. Catch yourself each time your mind begins to wander. Take thorough notes so that you can feel involved in the lecture. Observe the lecturer's style to determine what cues, such as tone of voice, speed, and volume, indicate when specific material is important. Above all, work on your attitude. Rethink unproductive classroom habits and resolve to improve.

Actively listening to history lectures is in principle the same as reading, evaluating evidence, and making an argument. In each case, it is essential to take in important details and make them part of a meaningful whole.

You may encounter lectures that are rambling and unfocused. If a lecture seems uninteresting, remember these two things: (1) you need the information to do well in the course, and (2) your participation in class can improve the lecture. Try to connect yourself mentally with the speaker. Answer a question or two that the instructor throws out to the class, or make a thoughtful comment about the lecture subject. Your feedback may inspire the instructor to become more animated and to speak more effectively.

WAYS TO ENHANCE LEARNING FROM LECTURES

1. Get enough sleep so that you can concentrate during lectures.
2. Don't let hunger interfere with your listening skills.
3. Arrive in class with enough time to settle in, copy the outline, and get focused before the lecture starts.
4. Stay actively involved with the lecture and do not put your brain on automatic pilot.
5. Pay attention to cues in the lecturer's tone, speed, volume, and gestures that can tell you what is most important.

Reporters' Techniques: Organizing as You Listen

Like newspaper reporters on assignment, active listeners are constantly looking for answers to their own questions, searching for the big picture, and organizing details. Reporters always look for stories, not just isolated facts but meaningful patterns of events as well. History, being made of stories, lends itself very well to this approach.

The essential task of the reporter is to ask questions. Even in situations where reporters may not be able to pose direct questions, the questions they have in mind guide their constant search for answers. This strategy works for history students, too.

For example, a student may come to a lecture on nineteenth-century imperialism with questions such as the following: What gave European nations the military advantage in their contacts with the rest of the world? How did the encounter between European and non-European peoples differ in various parts of the world? In the "IPSO" structure suggested in the last chapter, the question can pose the issue that the lecture answers.

Also like a reporter, be on the lookout for the big picture that gives meaning to the individual pieces. In a course on modern American history, for example, the civil rights groups of the 1950s would almost certainly be one of the important topics to be covered. Thus, if part of a lecture is devoted to the Birmingham bus boycott, be sure to think about this event in the context of the larger issue of the struggle for civil rights.

Suppose you were listening to a lecture on the Scientific Revolution. If you listen passively, you are apt to hear a rather boring catalogue of names, dates, and discoveries. Why not act as if you were a reporter on the hunt for a story, and turn the facts of the lecture into parts of an exciting news story. See the material as a grand drama, in which one view of the world replaces another and supporters of the old order clash with those committed to change. Or, turn what you hear into a mystery and imagine what clues scientist-detectives are gathering to support the new science.

■

Personal Learning Questions

Do you come to a lecture with important questions about the material that is being studied? Are you searching for the "big picture" when you listen to a lecture? Are you looking for appropriate bits of evidence, which you could use to support an argument?

■

When to Take Notes

Taking notes is the best way to preserve the information from a lecture. No matter how attentively and enthusiastically students listen, after a short time they will forget half of what they heard. After a week, most will remember only very general points and perhaps a novel detail or two. If you doubt this, try to recall the specific content of an informational television program you watched a week ago.

Therefore, you will need to take notes, but with as little distraction as possible from your comprehension of the lecture. If you try to write down every word the instructor utters, you are likely to fall behind and lose sight of the big picture. You must make decisions about what to record and what to let pass. Using questions to focus yourself and listening in terms of story lines will help you know when to take notes.

How to Take Notes

Find out what method of taking notes works best for you. Talk to others and experiment with various methods. You will need to develop an understandable shorthand as well as a way to organize information on the page so that it is accessible to you later.

Reporters commonly use narrow writing pads that measure about three inches across, moving their hand rapidly down the page and flipping pages as they go along. This simple measure can significantly reduce the fatigue of prolonged note taking. We recommend that you use a regular size notebook, but mark off a part of the page. If you use only part of a page, you can go back later and write in subject headings, related ideas, or references to the readings.

Organizing your notes as you write will help you to remain attentive and active. When you hear the same words over and over, save time and energy by minimizing the number of letters that you have to write down. You can speed up your note taking by using a personal shorthand of abbreviations and symbols for frequently used words. Some common abbreviations are shown here.

COMMON ABBREVIATIONS

w = with
(-) = between
< = less than
> = more than
~ = or
→ = to or toward
C = century
d = died
b = born
? = question
@ = all
← = from

You can also use this kind of shorthand for terms that pertain specifically to the subject matter of history. Below are some **historical abbreviations** that you might find useful in your history course.

HISTORICAL ABBREVIATIONS

ps = peasant
wr = worker
rev = revolution
Gk = Greek
med = medieval
Ref = Reformation
IR = Industrial Revolution
AR = American Revolution
CW = Civil War
WWI = World War I
WWII = World War II
ar = aristocrat or aristocratic
mc = middle class
anc = ancient
Rm = Rome or Roman
Ren = Renaissance
FR = French Revolution

Using Lecture Notes Later

Many students assume that note taking is over as soon as the class ends. On the contrary, if you go back over your lecture notes as soon as possible, you can add details that you failed to write down, rethink the basic concepts of the lecture, and in effect imprint the material more securely in your long-term memory.

Throughout the semester, review all your lecture notes and relate them to other aspects of the course. Take notes on your notes, adding headings, summaries, new ideas, and references to relevant material in the readings. At times, you will want to reread notes in great detail. On other occasions, skimming will be sufficient to reinforce your learning.

In addition, reviewing your notes gives you an opportunity to evaluate the methods you are using to take notes. When you go back over your notes, determine whether or not they convey the information you need. If you find them short on details or fuzzy on the big ideas, think about how you can change your note-taking style.

Note Taking in Collaboration

Throughout both your personal and professional lives, you will be spending much of your time operating in groups. Unfortunately, in most history courses the ideal of the rugged and isolated individualist still reigns. However, by tapping the enormous potential for human co-operation, you can achieve your goals in class and at the same time make the experience more pleasurable.

One strategy for handling lectures is to form a small group whose purpose is **collaborative note taking.** Members of this group take the best notes possible during class and then meet some time after class to compare, clarify, and exchange their notes. Members of collaborative note-taking groups may take turns preparing a master set of combined notes for each lecture.

Collaborative note-taking groups have the important advantage of engaging students in discussion and mutual teaching of the material in the lectures. Comprehension of both the textbook and the lectures is always enhanced through discussion with others.

■

PERSONAL LEARNING QUESTIONS

How often do you review your notes between a lecture and the next exam? Do you ever compare notes with other members of the class?

■

A Tale of Two Roommates

Doug and Mark have been roommates since the beginning of the se-mester, and tension has been building between them. Everything that one did seemed to irritate the other. The night before an important lec-ture, Mark came in at 3:00 A.M., which disturbed Doug. The next morn-ing, neither person was in the best of moods, and they had a fight about the telephone bill. Doug finally broke it off, grabbed breakfast, and then headed for the lecture.

When Doug got to class, he was still disturbed by the argument. He was also a bit sleepy. However, breakfast was beginning to kick in, and because he had arrived in class a few minutes early, he had time to calm down and transfer his attention from his personal life to the course. He took a moment to copy the outline from an overhead transparency (see below) and to orient himself to the issues in the course.

THE INDUSTRIAL REVOLUTION

I. The Nature of the Revolution
   A. Enormity of Change
   B. Changes in Production
      1. Adam Smith's Pin Factory
      2. Impact of Division of Labor
   C. Changes in Consumption
   D. Changes in Society
   E. Change Across Time and Geography
II. The Problem of Interpretation
   A. Complexity of Event
   B. Example of Historical Judgment
   C. Problems with Traditional Interpretations
III. Factors to Consider
   A. Religious/Cultural Factors—Weber Thesis
   B. Population Increase
   C. Agricultural Revolution
   D. Entrepreneurs and Capital
   E. Feedback Processes

Doug had already formed a general overview of the course from the syllabus and the textbook table of contents, so he knew that the Industrial Revolution was a central issue in the course and that he had better pay particular attention to this lecture. He had also already done the reading assignment for the week, so he had an overview of early industrialization. When he went over the outline, he already knew who Adam Smith was and what the Agricultural Revolution was, and he had even looked up the word *entrepreneur* in the dictionary when he encountered it in the textbook.

While the lecturer was adjusting the microphone around her neck, Doug thought about what he needed to get out of the lecture. There were several topics in the reading he had not completely understood, and he hoped the lecture would clarify these. He was, for example, uncertain how the Industrial Revolution had changed methods of industrial production, and he hoped that section I.B. of the outline would explain this. In addition, there were several large questions concerning the Industrial Revolution he knew he would have to be able to answer before the next exam: What were the primary characteristics of the Industrial Revolution? What factors contributed to its creation? Where and when did it start? What impact did it have? How did it affect various groups in society?

By the time the lecturer's microphone was connected and her lecture notes were spread out on the podium, Doug had made a complete mental transition to the course material. The morning's argument with Mark was now tucked away in his mind, and he was prepared to listen to the introduction, during which the instructor provided an overview of the material to be covered.

The instructor spoke rapidly, but because Doug had already marked off a narrow column in the middle of each page of his notebook, he could write quickly enough to keep pace with her. He had developed a set of abbreviations to further speed up his note taking. As he listened and wrote, Doug made an effort to distinguish between important concepts and examples. He had already observed that his instructor generally spoke loudly and slowly when she was presenting major concepts, so he had an external set of cues to indicate what was important.

At this point Mark, who was taking the same class, came into the room and sat down. For a moment, Doug's attention shifted back to their earlier argument. He replayed the tapes, imagining all the clever and cutting comments he should have made. After a couple of minutes, he snapped out of his trance and remembered that he was in a lecture and was supposed to be taking notes. He turned his attention back to the instructor just as she was saying " … destroyed the fabric of premodern society. The movement into the cities ripped apart many of the patterns of peasant culture, and the decline of the guilds eliminated vital social support systems in the cities." For a second, Doug panicked. Then, he remembered that he had already read about this in the textbook. Moreover, he had been listening for the story behind the details, and thus was in a position to pick up the thread of the lecture. Looking back at the outline, he guessed that the instructor was at point I.D., "Changes in Society." When she showed an overhead transparency of a map of Europe containing the dates that various areas had begun to industrialize, he knew that she was now at point I.E. "Change Across

Doug's Notes

I. THE NATURE OF THE I.R.
ENORMITY OF CHANGE
  Comparable with neolithic revolution
  (agriculture and metals)

  But it occurred in two or three generations

  Every aspect of life changed

CHANGES IN PROD.
  Enormous increase in prod.

  Adam Smith's pin factory
    Before, one worker made entire pin
      Guilds

  Now, work divided
    Many more pins made in day

  Principles: DIV. OF LABOR--SPECIALIZATION

IMPACT OF CHANGE IN METHOD OF PROD.
  Increase in prod.--lower unit costs
  Advantages of scale in larger fact.

  Movement from small shop to factory

    Guilds can't compete

    Separation of laborer from ownership

    Workers become employees, not members
      of social organization of guild

    Need larger market
      Move from local to regional to
        national market

    Need for transportation system,
      cities for workers, etc.

REV. IN LIFE RESULTS
Changes in consumption
  More goods--cheaper

Time and Geography." Doug thus was locked into the lecture again and could continue.

As soon as the lecture was over, he took just a moment to run his eyes back across his notes to reinforce his memory and to establish the main points in the lecture. A few days later, Doug met with three friends who got together once a week to study for their history course. They compared notes and produced a master copy, providing Doug with the material he had missed when he spaced out. They also speculated about what questions might be on the next exam, and how the material in this lecture might help them answer each question. Doug emerged from the meeting confident and ready for the exam. He would review again before the test, but he already had organized in his mind most of the concepts and details he would need.

Mark, as you probably have guessed, did not have it so easy. He stayed in his room stewing about his lousy roommate until he suddenly realized that he was late for class. By the time he got there, found a seat, copied the outline, and finally transferred his attention to the lecture, he had missed the introduction. The instructor was saying something about "guilds." Because Mark had not yet read the assignment for the week, he was not completely sure what guilds were. He did not think to look back at the outline, nor did he have any idea of the broader concepts contained in the lecture. So, he just tried to write down every word the instructor uttered. He could not write fast enough, however, so from time to time he lost track of what was being said. This produced gaps in his notes. Moreover, he was sleepy, hungry, and angry; bored by the lecture; and consumed with thoughts about his impossible roommate.

When the ordeal of the lecture was over, Mark closed his notebook and left the classroom as soon as possible. He did not look back at what he had written until a few days before the exam. What he found was a set of barely legible and disconnected bits of information. He memorized what he could understand, but he was forced to put in extra hours trying to coax enough information out of the textbook to face the exam.

On the exam, he was asked to discuss the manner in which changes in production methods during the Industrial Revolution led to radical changes in society. The pile of facts he had collected from the textbook and from his confused notes collapsed like a tower of cards, and he did poorly on the exam. Mark became angry and unfortunately did not use the experience to reevaluate his strategies for learning from lectures.

Those interested in our little drama for its own sake may be curious to know that this exam produced a change in living arrangements. When Mark found out that Doug had gotten a better grade on the exam with less study time, he accused the instructor of being unfair. Doug defended her, and the ensuing argument was so intense that the dorm assistant had to mediate. Within a week, the two former friends were living apart.

GETTING THE MOST OUT OF DISCUSSION

"Why should I waste my time listening to other students, who know no more about history than I do, or talking to myself about the subject, when I could be listening to the instructor, who supposedly is an expert in the field?" Such a response to class discussion is common among undergraduates, and you sometimes may have felt this way yourself. However, history instructors generally view lectures as a very limited form of instruction and believe that discussion plays a central role in learning.

This difference in seeing the value of discussion rests in large part on the assumptions you bring to learning history. If you view it essentially as a passive process in which the goal is to accumulate as many facts as possible, discussion probably will not seem important. If, by contrast, you see learning history as an active process, then the importance of discussion will be much clearer. Since the latter view reflects the view of most history teachers, it will be to your benefit to try to get the most out of discussion sessions.

Let us review briefly what you might hope to get out of a discussion. Here are a few of the possibilities.

Reinforcing Material Learned in Other Aspects of the Course—Material from lectures and the readings will generally be reprocessed during discussion. In most cases, you will be reminded of important information and concepts. You also will have a better sense of what parts of the readings and lectures are most important.

Hearing Concepts Expressed in Different Ways—We all have our own ways of explaining things. You may have heard your teacher present an idea a half-dozen times and yet find that it sinks in only after one of your classmates expresses it in slightly different terms.

Restating Concepts in Your Own Words—It has frequently been argued that you do not understand something until you have taught it to someone else. Discussion forces you out of your isolation. You must put what you know into words. When this works easily, you have reinforced and clarified the learning process. When you discover that it is difficult to express certain concepts, you have received a crucial warning that this material needs more work.

Practicing the Creation of Interpretations and Defending Them with Evidence and Logical Arguments—If you are going to present and defend interpretations on exams or papers, you will need practice. Discussion provides ample opportunities for this. You will be able to formulate interpretations, to develop supporting arguments, to marshal evidence, and to test your arguments against conflicting positions.

Improving Your Oral Communication Skills—Of all the skills you learn in college, speaking is almost certainly the one you will use most frequently. Most classroom settings provide a relatively stress-free environment in which you can perfect your ability to present and defend positions orally. The experience you gain here may be crucial when you are called on to explain and support a particular policy to a future employer.

Learning to Work in a Group—Most of the activities of a student are rather solitary ones. Discussion may be the only part in a history course in which you work with others. In today's world, where committees and work groups generate most decisions, learning the dynamics of group interaction is absolutely crucial, and classroom discussions provide a particularly useful place to explore these interactions.

Developing Your Own Positions on Crucial Issues—Discussion provides you with the chance to think aloud about issues that are of importance to you and to see how others respond to your ideas. It gives you an opportunity to entertain perspectives you may not have considered and to develop arguments to defend those you already hold.

Learning What it Feels Like to Do History—Regardless of how actively you respond to lectures and textbooks, there still is something passive in these methods of learning. In a discussion, everyone is a historian, analyzing data, presenting hypotheses, and evaluating evidence and arguments.

Achieving Academic Success—Remember that in many courses, participation in class discussion plays a major role in determining one's grade. Even when this is not the case, the impression you make in class may have an impact on the way your instructor judges your performance in other aspects of the course. And, finally, the impression you make on your instructor may make it easier to get strong letters of recommendation for graduate school or for jobs.

Having Fun—Discussion can be the most enjoyable part of a course. If you throw yourself into the process, you may be surprised how much you begin looking forward to class.

■

Personal Learning Questions

What has been your attitude in the past towards discussion? What things might you get out of discussion in the future? What would you like to gain from the discussions in your current history course?

Preparing for Discussion

Successful participation in discussion depends in large part on what you do before you arrive. There are, of course, clever talkers who will speak on any topic whether or not they know something about it. However, their credibility with both the instructor and other students generally begins to wear thin quite soon.

To be a true participant in discussion, you must be informed. You must have completed the reading assignment and attended the lecture. If you have completed only part of the assignment, you may find yourself unwilling to comment for fear that something on the last page of the reading will make your point seem stupid.

It also helps to process the material before you go to class. Think about the major issues raised in the lectures and readings. Were there controversies during the period you are studying that are apt to be a focal point for discussion? If, for example, you are studying the introduction of Buddhism into China, it would be wise to think about how the values and assumptions of the new religion differed from the Confucian and Taoist traditions already present, and how these religious groups might have interacted. Perhaps you can compare the various ways that historians have interpreted specific developments. Similarly, you may have had a strong reaction to the issues raised in the course and wish to prepare specific questions or arguments to be discussed in class.

If you have thought about such matters even for a few minutes before class, you will be way ahead of most of your classmates. Perhaps more important, though, you will have come a long way toward preparing yourself to use the **dynamics of discussion.**

■

PERSONAL LEARNING QUESTIONS

What can you do before your next discussion that will help you to use the class to achieve your goals more effectively? What should you think about before the next discussion in order to be more prepared to participate?

■

The Dynamics of Discussion: Make Sure You Talk

Many students fail to take full advantage of discussion because they decided at some point in their lives that they are not the kind of people who can speak up in class. Sometimes, students are just in the habit of being passive in discussion and never think of taking part. In other cases, a crushing response from a clumsy or vindictive teacher has left emotional scars that make it difficult to speak up.

If you feel (and act) this way, you are cheating yourself out of an important part of the course for which you paid. The students who are using the course to develop their communication abilities will have an advantage over you in future life situations. Moreover, their opinions and positions are being expressed and listened to, whereas yours are not.

How can you go about breaking down such limiting patterns? One way is to commit yourself to making a single comment in the next discussion, no matter what. This is generally easier if you have gone over the readings and lectures thoroughly and have a clear grasp of the major issues. Thinking in advance about topics likely to surface can help, and at first you may even want to formulate two or three general comments that you can throw in whenever appropriate.

Because you are trying to acquire a behavior that will likely help you throughout your life, you need to concentrate as much energy as possible on developing new ways of acting in class. Even if you don't speak up at first, imagine how it would feel if you did. Before class, envision yourself during the next hour. Then, when you are in class, think about yourself as someone who might make a contribution. And, at the end of the class, look back over the period and note when you might have said something but did not. Also notice whether the ceiling falls in on other students whose comments are a little off the mark. Remember, the point is not to destroy the behavioral patterns you have already built up, but rather to add the ability to take part in class discussion *when you decide that you want to*. You still will be able to choose to remain silent, even after you have enhanced your ability to participate.

If, however, your actual involvement in discussion does not seem to be increasing, you may wish to talk with your instructor. He or she may make it easier for you to enter discussion or may be willing to accept some other form of expression, such as a journal in which you write down your reactions to the readings and/or the discussion.

The Dynamics of Discussion: Don't Talk Too Much

A reluctance to leap into discussion is not, however, the only problem students may have. Some students may talk too much. A discussion is a complex social "game," and it is played by rules, even if those rules are not written down anywhere. If students interrupt other members of the class, make insulting comments, or completely dominate discussion, they have broken the rules as much as if they had fouled in a basketball game. Such behavior may seem like fun at the time, but it prompts negative reactions in other students and in faculty. Much worse, a habit of interrupting or dominating a discussion can be disastrous in personal and professional life.

Moreover, dominating discussion tends to short-circuit the free flow of ideas and arguments and thus eliminate much of the benefit of this part of the course. The knowledge and views of a wide range of classmates is a crucial resource. The student who is pushed out of discussion while taking a moment to think about a question may be precisely the one to make an important contribution.

Most students who are involved in such behavior are not vindictive or cruel; they are just unaware that these patterns are occurring or are unable to throw the off-switch in their vocal cords. Therefore, it is wise to monitor the way you take part in discussion. You might even want to place a check mark on a piece of paper every time you speak, and determine after class whether the frequency of your comments was appropriate.

If you think that you may be speaking too often, try to institute different patterns. Pause to be sure that you understand the question, to think of some specific evidence to support your point, to reflect on other positions, or to phrase your comment as effectively as you can. By speaking less often but more thoughtfully, you may find that your comments are more helpful to the discussion and that they better represent your ideas.

■

Personal Learning Questions

What kind of role have you generally played in class discussions in the past? What are the advantages and disadvantages of this kind of behavior? Would you like to be able to play different roles at least some of the time? If so, what steps might you take to learn a new role?

■

The Dynamics of Discussion: Stay on the Topic

It is always wise to make sure that your comments are on the mark. Discussion is a cooperative venture. Each comment should follow logically and thematically from the previous one. Staying on the topic at hand is a difficult task, one that requires skills that are increasingly important in the modern workplace. Therefore, it will be well worth your time to devote a little care to developing this ability.

The most important part of this task is to make sure that you are in touch with the discussion. Stop every few minutes and summarize to yourself what has been said. Be sure that you know what the central issues are and that you understand what the last several speakers were trying to say. If the comments of another student or the instructor are not completely clear to you, it may be much more productive to ask for clarification than to try to make a comment yourself. You may find that you are not the only person who is confused.

Finally, it is important to make sure that the tone of your comments contributes to the free flow of the discussion. It is very important to question and challenge the comments of other students. It is not appropriate, however, to insult or dismiss the comments of other members of the class. Discussion is productive only when all participants feel safe from attack. Students should be free to explore ideas and lines of thought they may subsequently abandon. A constant threat of negative judgment most likely will discourage discussion. Unfortunately, instructors themselves occasionally operate in this fashion. In such cases, students in the class should try even harder to be mutually supportive.

Gender-Minority Issues in Discussion

Thus far we have talked about taking part in discussion from the perspective of the individual. Gender and minority status, however, may also shape the flow of discussion. Therefore, it is important to understand **gender-minority discussion issues.**

Studies by sociologists and educators consistently have demonstrated that gender has a major effect on how individuals perform in the classroom. Men, for example, tend to be much more vocal and may dominate discussion. They generally respond to questions more quickly and are much more apt to interrupt. Women, on the other hand, are more likely to think longer before they respond, and they tend to defer more readily to others.

These are, of course, only statistical tendencies. There are many members of each gender who do not fit this pattern. Don't be too quick to assume that you are atypical. Studies also have indicated that students—and faculty—often are unaware that they act according to gender stereotypes. Males often dominate, and females often yield, without noticing it.

Such patterns can greatly diminish the value of discussion for both men and women. Male competition for the floor can exclude those students, male and female, who like to think about an issue for a moment before they rush in. Such this haste can trivialize the discussion. Women who automatically defer to their more aggressive male peers may not share with the rest of the class perspectives that would be of great value.

Therefore, to get the most out of discussion and to become better prepared to operate in groups outside of class, pay attention to the way you participate in discussion. You probably have one role down pat already. Now is the time to discover other roles so that you can acquire the full set of interactive tools you need. If you find it easy and natural to move right in when a question is asked, try to hold back and learn from the other students. If it is natural for you to listen and to defer to the needs of others in the class, practice asserting yourself and making sure that your opinions get heard. In either case, you will be making an enormous contribution to the class and to your own development as a human being.

Similar problems can result from being a member of a racial or ethnic group that differs from the majority of the class. It is easy to feel excluded from the discussion if your experience has been different from that of your classmates or if they assume that it has. This feeling of being an outsider can be made even worse if you are singled out as a spokesperson for some group to which you belong. What could be more inhibiting that being heard as the voice of millions of people you have never met and with whom you may have little in common?

There is no simple solution to this problem. There are, however, a few things you can remember that should help. First, remind yourself that there is in fact no real "majority." What may appear to be a monolithic majority group is really divided by gender, class, status, national ancestry, family experience, and a multitude of other factors. Two students who are the youngest members of their families may share something important in common that each does not share with many other members of his or her own gender, race, or ethnic group. Thus, depending on the issue being discussed, you will find yourself sometimes in the majority and sometimes in the minority.

Second, it is important to understand how valuable difference is in the learning process. Throughout this textbook, we have stressed that the ability to see events from different perspectives is crucial for understanding the past. If a variety of experiences, perspectives, and values are represented in the class, each member has much more to gain and much more to give. Take advantage of this opportunity.

Finally, if you are uncomfortable being asked to speak for a larger group, express your discomfort. Make it clear, politely but firmly, that you are willing to speak only for yourself. This process of setting boundaries will probably earn you respect at the same time that it creates a space in which you can comfortably participate in class.

It is important to keep these considerations in mind even if you represent an easily identifiable majority in a particular class. Don't speak for all members of your group, and don't expect others to speak for theirs. Remember that it is the sharing of the particular experiences and insights of the individual that will ultimately teach everyone the most.

Thus far we have been discussing gender-minority issues that pertain only to interactions among students. Such issues, however, can also affect student-teacher interactions. Studies have demonstrated that some instructors unconsciously call on white males more frequently when several members of the class have volunteered to speak. Others, as we indicated earlier, tend to ask students to speak for the larger groups with which they are identified. At the most disturbing end of the spectrum, faculty members may express racial or gender stereotypes, or they may use humor in a manner that makes students feel uncomfortable.

Such behavior is, of course, highly inappropriate. You have the right to expect respect and a positive learning environment in every class you take. If you are faced with such behavior, the first step is to recognize that the fault lies with the faculty member and the society that produces such behavior. It is not your fault, and you should not allow it to undercut your own sense of worth. Talking to other students or to a faculty member whom you trust may serve to raise the consciousness of those around you. Unless you are convinced that such a move would produce reprisals, speak to the erring faculty member (outside of class). You probably will get better results if you concentrate on expressing how you felt rather than on what you perceive the teacher has done. If you do not receive an appropriate response from your teacher, or if the behavior is interfering with your learning, then it is appropriate to report your experiences to university authorities, just as you would report sexual harassment or a racially motivated attack. Try to be as explicit as you can and, if possible, provide a log or journal in which you have written down examples of the inappropriate behavior as it occurred over time. Even if action is not taken immediately on your complaint, you are standing up for your rights as a student, and the information you provide eventually may be useful in demonstrating a pattern of behavior in this particular faculty member.

■

PERSONAL LEARNING QUESTION

How has your gender, race, or ethnicity affected your interactions in class, both with other students and with your instructor?

■

Discussion and Note Taking

Students often are uncertain how they should go about retaining what they have learned from discussion. There is no absolute rule about note taking, but it is generally unwise to take verbatim notes during a discussion. Writing will tend to isolate you from what is going on, and focusing entirely on recording the thoughts of others will keep you from exploring your own ideas.

On the other hand, it may be useful to come out of discussion with some record of the proceedings. You may wish to experiment with a very different kind of note taking than you use in lectures. Leave a pad of paper open on your desk with a pen next to it. From time to time, write down a word or two that can later serve to bring material from the discussion back into your active memory. You may also want to write down particularly interesting ideas or interpretations.

After the discussion has ended, look back over these notes and write down what you think was important in the discussion. Observe the positions taken by various students and the arguments they used to support their positions. If some topics were unclear to you, note that you need to explore these topics further in the textbook or to talk to the instructor about them. These notes can be very useful when you are preparing for an exam.

You may wish to use a tape recorder during discussions. Always be sure to get permission from the instructor before taping either discussions or lectures. Also, remember that the tape recorder is there to help you participate more actively, not relax. During the discussion itself, focus on the flow of the argument and on points where you can contribute to the debate. Later, replay the tape and take notes, but do not transcribe the tape verbatim. Try to summarize the main points of various speakers, and at the end of each line of discussion formulate your own position on a particular issue.

Role Playing

In some courses, you may experience new forms of interaction among students. Rather than simply discussing a series of questions, you may be asked to play a specified role. Such **role playing** may be as simple as a staged debate on a particular topic or it may involve a complex simulation of the life of a particular era. You might, for example, be asked to play the role of a nineteenth-century industrial worker while other students represent middle-class factory owners. Similarly, the class might be asked to relive the roles of Catholics and Protestants in the Reformation, of abolitionists and slaveholders in mid-nineteenth-century America, or of native peoples and European colonialists.

Some students do not take such activities seriously, but role playing can contribute greatly to your learning process. Any event or era can be understood only from the multiple viewpoints of various groups. The actions of these groups and the conflicts among them provided the impetus for historical change. To understand the past, you need to see it from the perspective of the individuals who lived in the past. Role playing provides a particularly powerful means of doing this.

Therefore, throwing yourself into a role-playing exercise may be one of the most valuable things you do in a semester. It is not always easy, however. To recreate a character from the past, you have to know a lot about the time, place, and situation of that character. In short, you have to know the material in the readings and lectures. But, beyond that, you have to use your imagination to occupy a role that is not your own. You can't assume a world view like your own. You must project yourself into the world of other people and think about how that world affected their attitudes and opinions, their relations to other groups, and even their sense of self. How did these individuals live? What did they know? How did they react to the basic issues of their time and to the other groups of the period? How does it feel to stand in their shoes? Think of role playing as a kind of psychological time travel. It can involve you in critical reading and thinking at a deeper level than other forms of study.

Through role playing, you will gain not only a much greater understanding of the period, but also of the ways human beings operate in general. As a result, your capacity for empathy will increase. The ability to empathize with the experiences and viewpoints of others will enhance virtually any personal or career goal.

Forming a Study Group

Some history courses do not include discussion. Lack of discussion in your class does not mean that you are excluded from the benefits of interacting with others. Get together with classmates and form your own **study group.** Even if discussion is part of the class, you may still find it useful to create a group to go back over the basic issues in the course. This will give you an opportunity to test your arguments and to listen to the positions of others. You can also explore some of the issues raised by readings and lectures. If you wish, you can even play the roles of various groups from the period to get a better sense of how the society functioned.

Forming an effective study group doesn't just happen. You must carefully consider the size of the group, the criteria for membership, the procedures that govern the group while in session, and the responsibility of each member to the group. Below are guidelines for these factors. Try them out!

Size of Group   There is no hard-and-fast rule for size of group, but groups of three to five have been proven effective in many settings. A minimum of three allows for three perspectives, which is a good number for negotiations. If a group is larger than five, there may be some who do not participate as much as others. Also, the logistics of getting together gets more difficult. A larger group can function, of course, if all members are equally committed and active.

Membership of Group   Some ground rules for joining and remaining in the group should be set. The most important is commitment. Each member should pledge to complete all tasks set for each group meeting—all reading, note taking, prediction of examination questions, etc. Coming to one meeting unprepared should put the member on probation. If the offense is repeated, the member should agree to leave the group. Moreover, each member should commit to discussing the course material, not to using the time as a bull session.

Also, members should agree that equal participation is important and help each other achieve that aim. If a talkative member is using too much time, that person should yield the floor to others. If a shy member doesn't talk enough, others should help that person with directed questions and encouragement. Finally, a group can and probably should include a range of abilities in the area of history. A knowledgeable member can learn a lot by explaining to a less knowledgeable member. A student less certain of historical knowledge can help the group by demanding very clear and complete explanations.

Structure of Group   Each meeting should be set up with an agenda, time frame, and designated roles. Responsibilities within this structure should rotate among group members.

In terms of agenda, specific tasks should be set at the end of each meeting for the next meeting. For example, each group member could agree to cover a portion of the reading assignment in detail and produce an elaborate set of notes for the group. The next meeting then would involve putting the "jigsaw" together after everyone had read the whole assignment. Or, each member could predict and answer an essay question for a session devoted to preparing for an exam.

In terms of time frame, set a specific time and place for the next meeting, with all members entering the information on their calendars as a serious commitment. One person in the group might take on the task of reminding the other members a day or two in advance. It is also a good idea to meet at least once a week for two hours so that the group gets in the habit of devoting this time to studying collaboratively.

In terms of designated roles, each group should have a discussion leader, a note-taker, and an agenda monitor, who makes sure the group stays on task and sets an agenda for the next meeting before disbanding. These roles should be rotated so every member serves each function the same amount of time.

Tasks   The study group can accomplish a wide range of tasks. These include discussion of readings and lectures, review for exams, brainstorming for papers and other projects, peer response and editing of papers, and formulation of key questions to ask the instructor.

As should be clear by now, discussion is a marvelous tool that you can use to achieve your goals. Your knowledge of the past will become active instead of passive. You will have an opportunity to restate the material in your own words, to test arguments, and to benefit from the insights of your fellow students. You will almost certainly find that this has all been useful at examination time, and it will also make the experience of learning more pleasurable. You might even learn to learn without an instructor and succeed in making your entire life a learning process.

APPLICATION EXERCISES

1. How do you know if you're ready to hear a lecture? Each time you go to class, ask yourself if you have

   - gotten enough sleep and nutrition to be alert.

   - checked the syllabus for the topic and reading assignment related to the lecture.

   - read the assignment.

   - taken reading notes to relate to the lecture.

   - prepared and collected the materials you need for note taking.

   - given yourself time to arrive at the lecture before it begins.

   - selected a seat that is at optimum distance from the lecturer for you.

   - focused your mind on today's topic and eliminated all distractions.

- thought about what you want to get out of the lecture.

2. Pair up with someone in the course and form the habit of getting together as soon as possible after the lecture to compare notes.

3. Compare your listening and note-taking behaviors across all your courses. In what course do you have the easiest time comprehending and taking notes from lectures? In what course do you have the most difficult time? What factors under your control affect your experience in each course?

4. As a student in the course, you contribute to the overall quality of the learning situation. Following are some ways in which you can make a positive contribution. Try to think of them while you are attending your next history lecture.

    - Arrive on time and be composed before the lecture begins.

    - Sit close enough to the lecturer to make eye contact.

    - Maintain an alert posture, occasionally using body language to give feedback to the lecturer (e.g., nodding your head and showing a quizzical expression).

    - Don't allow students around you to distract you or engage you in conversation during the lecture.

    - Keep your attention on the lecture throughout the period.

    - Wait until the lecturer is finished before you close your notebook and prepare to leave.

    - Go up to the lecturer immediately after class if you have questions.

5. Keep a record of how many times you make a contribution to discussion. Compare it to the number of times your classmates make comments. Decide whether you tend to be an active participant or a passive participant.

6. Before the next class, think of a question that would help you and others in the class understand the material better. Pledge to ask that one question even if you say nothing more during the class.

7. After you are able to ask at least one good question in each session, move on to answering someone else's question. Pick a section of the reading assignment that you understand particularly

well. When someone poses a question on that section, offer a knowledgeable reply. This will build your confidence in yourself.

8. Talk to the instructor. A good way to "break the ice" when you have been silent up to now is to talk to the instructor individually, either after class or during office hours. Once you have done that, chances are good that the instructor will direct a question to you or at least look at you expectantly during the discussion. You will feel drawn in and find responding much more comfortable.

9. Shyness in a group may result from feeling like a stranger. Get to know others in the class and perhaps form a study group with some. Again, you will find participating in class much more comfortable when you know you have supporters in the room.

TERMS TO KNOW

collaborative note taking
dynamics of discussion
gender-minority discussion issues
historical abbreviations
role playing
study group

CHAPTER 7

PREPARING FOR AND TAKING EXAMS

- *How can you begin preparing for exams as soon as the course starts?*

- *How can you create an effective exam-preparation system from the reading, listening, discussing, and note-taking strategies presented in this book?*

- *What can you do after an exam to get a head start on the next one?*

- *Do you have greater strengths in answering certain kinds of exam questions? Are there kinds of questions that are especially difficult for you? How would you explain these strengths and weaknesses?*

- *How can you adapt your semester-long study strategies to the questions likely to appear on exams?*

Many people associate exams with anxiety, but this is not necessarily a bad thing. In moderate amounts, anxiety can play a useful role in our mastery of knowledge. Anxiety serves as a reminder of something important to us that deserves our attention. As you become familiar with the study of history, develop effective strategies for reading, listening, and discussing, and, as your critical abilities sharpen, your anxiety will grow into confidence. We all need a nudge to get us going.

Excess anxiety, however, can be detrimental to your performance on an exam. Therefore, you must remind yourself that an exam is not a judgment of you as a human being. The most any examination can do is to evaluate your performance at a specific task on a specific day according to specific criteria. A student once described taking exams as "pulling up a plant by the roots to examine its growth." Every exam takes just a sample of what you know. The instructor assumes that this sample is representative of your knowledge, but it may not really reflect your understanding of the subject as a whole. It is always your performance at a particular moment that is being measured, not your potential for growth or your absolute worth as a person.

Of course, your success on a test may have concrete consequences for you in the real world. The results may say something about your learning strategies, whether you devoted an adequate amount of time to studying, or how motivated you are to learn about history. There are specific strategies you can use to maximize your performance on exams. **Exam preparation strategies** refer to your study choices up to the moment the exam begins. This section will guide you in studying for exams. The next section, **exam performance strategies**, will focus on what to do during the actual testing period.

PREPARATION STRATEGIES

You can get a higher grade without increasing the amount of time you spend studying if you consciously develop effective study methods. The central factor in such strategies is organization. You must organize your time and energy in the days before an exam as well as throughout the whole semester. Short-term and long-term efficiency will boost your success. How can you make the best use of the last two or three days before the exam? Should you cram? Reread? Review? Sit back and relax? The kind of thinking you do a couple of days before the examination, whether clear and focused or fuzzy and vague, is a key factor in how well you will do on the exam.

How Cheryl Studied for Her Exam

Here is the story of a student who failed to make effective use of the crucial period before an exam. Having done all her homework, Cheryl believed she understood and remembered the material in the course. Her performance on the test, however, was miserable. To understand what happened, we will review her actions in the days before the Monday exam.

Saturday was Cheryl's "leisure day" and she chose not to study. Because she had nothing in particular planned for Sunday, this seemed like a good time to get lots of reviewing done. On Saturday night, she had a late date with her boyfriend and didn't get to sleep until 2:30 or 3:00 A.M. Sunday morning she devoted to breakfast and church. Finally, she settled down to study, but after half an hour she felt sleepy and napped for a couple of hours. When she woke up, it was time to get ready for dinner. Afterward, she studied for an hour or so, but she still felt tired and dozed off again. Looking back on Sunday, Cheryl had the impression that she had tried to study all day. In reality, she had spent most of the day eating, sleeping, and spending time with others.

On Monday morning, she headed straight to her English composition class. At 9:30, an hour before the exam, she went to the student union building with good intentions to study. She did spend a little time looking back over the textbook, but a friend joined her and she ended up talking about other things. When she arrived at history class and saw the test questions, she felt completely unprepared. Her mind went blank. She failed the exam, even though she had done average or better on previous exams in the course. What went wrong?

Cheryl's short-term study strategies were deficient. Underlying her actions before the exam was this basic rule: fit studying in whenever there is a gap in my schedule. This flawed method allowed other activities to crowd out her study time. She also failed to set aside a time early in the preparation period to review the material and determine what she needed to study. Had she spent an hour on Saturday morning developing answers to hypothetical test questions, she would have realized that she needed to designate a significant, uninterrupted block of time to review. Cheryl's central problem was time management. Even when she did study, her use of time was inefficient. Just turning pages is not an effective way to prepare. Cheryl's example shows that it is not enough to absorb information at an earlier time. You must actively reorganize your thoughts before the exam to make them accessible during the exam.

Effective Short-Term Study Strategies

There are a number of short-term strategies you can use to prepare for exams. Here are some strategies that you might find particularly effective.

- Attend review sessions offered by the instructor.
- Investigate exams from former years of the same course.
- Review your last exam, noting the grader's suggestions for improvement.
- List important concepts, people, places, and events that might appear on short-answer identifications and consider them in the context of the course.
- Map out the major themes of the course.
- Create hypothetical essay questions, outline your answers, and include supporting details.
- Identify material in the course that is still not clear.
- Explain the basic concepts of the course to friends who are not taking it.
- Meet with other students in the class to discuss what questions to expect on the exam and possible answers.
- Insist that you remain focused on the test material, whether alone or in a study group.

■

Personal Learning Questions

How successful have you been in the past at managing your study time in the period immediately before tests? What might you do to use your time more wisely?
What kinds of short-term study strategies have you used in the past? What new strategies do you think would be helpful for the next test in your history course?

■

Long-Term Preparation

What you do in the days immediately before an exam is important, but not as important as what you do throughout the semester. Ongoing, consistent study provides the groundwork that makes pre-test studying easier, more effective and, in fact, less urgent. You may benefit as much from a couple of hours of review as you formerly did from many hours of frantic cramming. If Cheryl had been preparing in the preceding weeks, she probably would have received a better grade, even if she was distracted.

Creating Your Own Study Guide

Your study habits will be enhanced when you learn to read actively, take notes well, annotate important points in the text, and practice getting the most out of discussion. In addition, it may help you to create a guide that brings together all your study activities throughout the semester. Such a **study guide** should match your own learning style and the particular course for which it is designed. Organizing your ideas in order to create a study guide is a valuable experience, and you will have the guide to use as a resource.

Jill's Story   Jill created a personalized study guide to accompany the same course and prepare for the same test that Cheryl failed. She recognized that reviewing for an exam doesn't work if you rely solely on memory, so she made a written record of all that transpired in the course. She then organized this record into a usable system that included her lecture notes, reading notes, class handouts, past exams, and a list of her own ideas. Each week throughout the semester, Jill scheduled time to add new material and review her study guide. Here are some of the innovative ways she developed her study guide.

Constructing Super Maps. Jill drew maps to conceptualize historical junctures and unified these to create a **super map** to give herself an overall perspective.

Enhancing with Note Cards. Jill augmented her super-map study by adding the note cards she had written about the readings. This helped her visualize how written statements apply to parts of the super map.

Recording New Ideas. Jill kept a running log of insights that occurred to her as she reviewed the material. From time to time, she would combine these ideas with older material to create conceptual maps and diagrams. She wrote down new material on concept cards.

Anticipating Exam Questions. Test files revealed that exams in the course were likely to contain three short identification questions and one comprehensive essay question. Knowing this, Jill began to formulate possible questions to answer for practice. To practice answering identification questions, she jotted down key words. For each essay question, she constructed a brief outline including the major issues she wanted to cover and some supporting details she might use. Because she started early in the semester, more possibilities occurred to her and her answers matured.

If there isn't a public test file to check to find out the likely format of your instructor's questions, you should ask the instructor directly. Almost every instructor will describe the kinds of questions to expect on an upcoming exam. If the information you receive from this request isn't enough, talk to people who have taken this course from this instructor in previous semesters.

Identifying Confusing Material.   When Jill began to restate course material in her own words, she sometimes discovered that she did not understand it as well as she had thought. To remedy this, she went back to the textbook, asked questions in class discussion, and asked for help from other students and the instructor. By so doing, she was able to clarify problems well before she was faced with exam questions.

The Successful Outcome   As you might guess, Jill aced the exam that Cheryl failed. How they prepared for the test made all the difference. While Cheryl lamely leafed through the material, Jill studied actively. Jill's self-made study guide helped her identify and define her study goals. While she studied, she questioned, mapped out things, and wrote down her ideas. It was especially helpful to cross-check separate parts of her study guide, such as note cards and maps or her lecture notes, against class handouts. These strategies automatically fixed the details of the course in her memory. They also systematized her knowledge so she could recall the right detail when needed.

ELEMENTS OF A PRODUCTIVE STUDY GUIDE

Lecture notes, dated and in chronological order, with annotations made in review sessions

Reading notes, consisting of chapter outlines and important points

Concept cards: set of 3" x 5" flash cards with a specific concept or topic written on each

Summary of major issues raised in class discussion, preferably written out after each class

Class handouts and supplementary material

Maps, perhaps a series of the same region demonstrating a sequence of historical events

Sample of exam from former semester, copied from a public test file

List of material that is unclear

Running list of your own questions and ideas in response to lectures, readings, and discussion

■

PERSONAL LEARNING QUESTIONS

What kinds of long-term exam preparations have you made in the past? What has been most successful?
Which strategies would you like to add in the future? What might you include in a study guide for your current history course?

■

PERFORMANCE STRATEGIES: TAKING THE TEST

The best way to drive away test anxiety is to be thoroughly prepared. You want to go into an exam with confidence. But, how do you deal with the on-the-spot anxiety of taking the exam? Success on examinations depends in part on your ability to perform well under stress. Rather than give way to panic, you must channel your energy onto focusing on the challenges.

First, take a deep, slow breath. Don't assume that you have to spend every minute answering questions, because it is not a waste of time to stop and consider how to proceed. In preparing for the exam, you will have gathered and organized information and anticipated questions. Now that you are actually taking the exam, you must still devote time to preparation, which includes making an overall assessment of the test in front of you and how you will get through all parts of it. However, you need to do this assessment efficiently and get on to answering questions energetically. You may have answered half of the multiple choice questions perfectly and written a brilliant response to the first two of the five steps required by an essay question, but if the bell rings before you finish you are in trouble. Remember, you are not judged on what you know, but on what you actually write down.

During an exam, you must devote a part of your brain to keeping track of the time. To alleviate panic every time you look at the clock, break up the task into small parts. Assign a certain number of minutes to each section, splitting essay questions into sections, too. Then stick to your schedule, obeying every section deadline. If you notice that you haven't completed something in the allotted time, summarize the rest of your ideas in a couple of sentences or jot down your preparatory outline using complete words. Leave space for the rest of your answer if you have time at the end to come back and finish it.

■

Personal Learning Questions

**Think back over your performance during exams in the past.
What strategies have worked well for you? What traps have you
fallen into?
What are the two or three things about taking a test that you
most want to remember the next time that you are in an exam
room? What can you do to make sure that you remember these
things under pressure?**

■

After the Exam

Many students believe that as soon as an exam is over, it is time to stop thinking about it. Others use the time after an exam to tell themselves how stupid they are. Neither strategy is very useful.

The period immediately after exams is, however, potentially one of the most important times in your academic career. Every exam that you take gives you vitally important information about your study strategies. Therefore, take a moment and think about what worked and what did not work, about what you would like to do the same next time and what you would like to do differently. And, after the test is returned, it may be valuable to meet with your instructor to get some pointers on how to improve your performance on the next test.

Hopefully, the more you perfect your study strategies, the more often you will leave an exam with the feeling that you made the best possible use of your time and knowledge. However, even under the best of circumstances, you will sometimes realize that you made a miscalculation somewhere along the way. Take in the information, decide what to change in your strategy, and realize that what you learned at that moment may be more important than anything that happened on the exam.

■

Personal Learning Questions

What steps can you take after the next exam to get as much feedback as possible concerning your study strategies? How can you be sure to incorporate into the next exam what you learn from your study strategies?

■

Also, remember that sometimes you will encounter an examination that is truly too long or too demanding. Although rare, there are instructors who try to design exams that only the most brilliant students can complete. If you are faced with such an exam, you should still feel good about having made your best effort to do well. In addition, the probability is high that your exam will compare favorably to those of other students in the class.

In the next section, the "anatomy" of history exam questions is examined in some detail. The insights you gain about different kinds of multiple choice questions, other short questions, and essay questions will enable you to devise both preparation strategies and test-taking strategies that will bring you close to your goal: an A on your next exam!

EXAM QUESTIONS

This section examines the various kinds of questions likely to appear on history exams. It takes skill to read complex questions. The better you are able to read such questions, the more time you'll have during the test for answering them.

Exam questions generally fall into two categories: *recognition* and *recall*. Both of these may entail a third "R," *reasoning*. Recognition questions, such as multiple-choice questions, ask you to select the correct answer from provided alternatives. Recall questions ask you to produce an answer yourself in either short or long form.

Multiple-Choice Questions

Multiple-choice questions assess a range of different things, from your comprehension of points in the material to your own understanding of interpretations. Always consider the purpose of the question when answering it.

In the simplest form of multiple-choice, **recall multiple-choice items** pose a query in the first part of the question and a list of seemingly possible responses in the second part. Following is an example of this type of multiple-choice question.

1. In the English Civil War, Cromwell led the New Model Army for

    a. the Stuarts.

    b. Parliament.

    c. the French.

    d. none of the above.

When considering the responses, it helps to narrow down the choices. In the preceding example, if you know Cromwell was English you can eliminate (c) the French. For every item you eliminate, you increase the probability of choosing the correct answer. Even if you are so familiar with the material that you zero in on the correct answer, it is a good idea to consider each and eliminate incorrect ones, because alternatives sometimes are designed to trick you.

Interpretive Multiple-Choice Questions

Not all multiple-choice questions aim at a simple repetition of factual details. Some focus on more complex issues, such as the interpretations presented in the readings. The following examples illustrate **interpretive multiple-choice items.**

2. In Long's account of American history, who or what was *most* responsible for the economic hardships so many people suffered during the 1930s?

   a. the rich industrialists and financiers who monopolized the wealth of America

   b. the Republican party, which had caused the Depression

   c. Franklin Delano Roosevelt, who had bungled the government's attempts to help its citizens

   d. the American people themselves for believing in a set of antiquated values

   e. greedy community merchants and bankers who had capitalized on their neighbors' hardships

3. According to Brinkley, the *most* significant difference between the ideology and behavior of Huey Long and Father Coughlin versus that of Adolf Hitler was

   a. their differing attitudes toward private property.

   b. their differing attitudes toward the suspension of civil and political liberties during a time of crisis.

   c. their differing stances on the importance and significance of individualism.

   d. their differing stances toward an idealized, traditional community.

   e. their differing attitudes toward ethnic and racial minorities.

In contrast to our first multiple-choice example, these two questions require more than just simple recall of facts. You must make a judgment, but one that is based on your interpretation of the readings, not on what *you* think sounds reasonable. The authors Long and Brinkley may have mentioned several of the interpretations listed as alternative answers. You must determine what the authors believed to be the *most* important factor contributing to the historical circumstance. For this kind of question, you need to have read the material critically to discern the authors' point of view.

In addition to readings, class lectures and discussions often form the basis of interpretive multiple-choice questions. Consider the following question.

4. In our class discussion of the infection rates at two Boston maternity hospitals in the late nineteenth century, we concluded that

   a. there was no difference in the infection rates of the two hospitals.

   b. there was a difference in infection rates, but the gender of the physicians had no impact on those rates.

   c. there was an indirect connection between the gender of the physicians and the infection rates.

   d. gender was a direct source of the difference because of superior male knowledge of germ theory.

   e. gender was a direct source of the difference because of superior female knowledge of germ theory.

Once again, the answer depends not on your memory of facts or your own interpretation, but rather on your understanding of the interpretation that predominated in the class discussion.

Other multiple-choice questions call for the test-taker's own judgment, based on careful critical reading and listening:

5. Historians have noted that Hitler manipulated the German people's sense of their own history to gain credence for his regime. What aspect of German history was most central to Hitler's message?

   a. Hitler's promise to end the oppression that had characterized the Kaiser's rule

   b. Hitler's promise to restore Germany to its former glory

   c. Hitler's promise to end the humiliation caused by the Allied treatment of Germany after World War I

   d. all of the above

   e. only b and c

This question asks you to decide which answer seems most likely to *you* based on your knowledge of the period. If you have understood the material in your readings and lectures, you can begin by eliminating (a), because you know that the goal of ending political oppression was not high on Hitler's list of priorities. In addition, you probably recognize that (b), the restoration of Germany's glory and (c), ending Germany's humiliation caused by the Treaty of Versailles, were so closely intertwined for German nationalists of the period that it would not make sense to say one was more important than the other. Therefore, on the basis of your own knowledge and reasoning, you can conclude that answer (e), only b and c, is the correct one.

As these examples demonstrate, careful reading is extremely important in answering multiple-choice questions. The following tips are suggested by Charles Brown and Royce Adams, respected researchers in the area of study skills.

Look for key words that will help determine the best answer. The following example shows the importance of key words.

6. The first exploration of new water routes to the east was undertaken by

   a. English adventurers.

   b. Portuguese navigators.

   c. Italian merchants.

   d. Spanish traders.

The key word here is "first." All of the groups listed took part in the exploration, but only one was the first to do so.

Watch out for negatives or other complexities of syntax. Consider this example.

7. Which of these factors did not contribute to the colonies' decision to declare independence?

   a. the great victory at Saratoga

   b. the British hiring of Hessian troops

   c. the publication of *Common Sense*

   d. the hope of an alliance with France

If you skipped over the word "not," you might have picked one of the three factors that did contribute.

Watch out for absolute terms such as "all," "none," "always," "never," and "only." These items are false or the incorrect choices in a multiple-choice test if any exceptions are present. And, since there usually are exceptions to any generalization, these words should also alert you to read cautiously. See, for example, the following question.

8. European conquest of Africa in the late nineteenth century

   a. met with no resistance from African peoples.

   b. could overpower most African resistance because of industrial technology.

   c. always found local elites to cooperate with European aims.

   d. all of the above.

Only the second of these answers does not include an absolute. Because there likely are some exceptions to (a) and (c), which negates (d) as well, only answer (c) can be correct.

Look for relativistic terms such as "sometimes," "often," "usually," and "most." These items call for judgments that are less certain but may tend more often to be true. Answering these questions may require a critical understanding of the material. Consider the following example.

9. In the medieval and early-modern periods in Europe, heretical religious movements

   a. usually featured political overtones.

   b. sometimes included political as well as religious claims.

   c. seldom addressed political issues.

   d. none of the above.

The structure of this question makes (d) an unlikely answer because any understanding of the material confirms a connection between heretical religion and politics, the issue being how strong the connection was. The other choices cover different possibilities. If you've done your reading, you'll decide (a) is your answer.

Students sometimes assume that multiple-choice questions are the easiest type of question to answer, but they can be quite demanding. In all recognition formats, the possibilities are controlled by the test writer. There is one answer that is correct and usually no way to argue for a different perspective.

HOW TO PERFORM WELL ON MULTIPLE-CHOICE TESTS

1. Determine which questions call for information about history and which call for information about interpretations of history.
2. Locate the key words in each question.
3. Notice if any questions use negatives or complex syntax that could lead you to misunderstand what is called for.
4. Identify any questions that use absolute terms such as all, none, always, never, and only and determine how these terms affect what is being asked.
5. Identify any questions that use relative terms such as sometimes, often, usually, and most and determine how these words affect the question.

True-False Questions

Like multiple-choice questions, true-false questions can seem deceptively simple. With these questions, however, you have to watch for tricky wording, such as qualifiers that render incorrect a seemingly correct statement. Take for example, the sentence "Bootleggers in the American Prohibition Era were always punished by law." Without the qualifier "always," this is a perfectly sound statement. As it stands, however, you would have to answer "false" if you read it on a true-false test.

Knowing the subject completely is crucial to answering true-false questions, because the statement is so isolated that nothing around it will give you a hint. When multiple-choice questions offer a list with several options, you automatically compare these options and possibly pick up on something you might have forgotten. Not so with true-false questions. If you don't remember what "bootleggers" were or what the "Prohibition Era" was, nothing else will tip you off.

You also can't compare qualifiers and choose, for example, whether bootleggers were sometimes, always, or never punished for their actions. Therefore, as you read the question, note qualifiers and be skeptical if they express absolutes. Also, remember that these questions are not asking for your opinion, but rather for the stance held by the textbook, the instructor, or the class consensus.

More than any other kind of exam question, true-false questions can make you feel exhilarated when you know the right answers. Plowing knowledgeably through a true-false section can really bolster your confidence in how well you covered the course material. Just remember to read the statements carefully.

Short-Answer Questions

Multiple-choice and true-false questions ask you to recognize the correct answer. In contrast, **short-answer questions,** sometimes called identifications or definitions, leave the response open-ended. You must recall and recount information associated with isolated items, essentially providing their context. Your written answer will be "short" in relation to an essay, ranging from a phrase or sentence to a few lines of description. Consider the following example from a midterm examination.

Identify (briefly tell *who* or *what*) and explain the *significance* of *five* of the following:

> Eiffel Tower
>
> Fashoda
>
> Sarajevo
>
> Cubism
>
> J. Dobson
>
> Triple Entente
>
> David Lloyd George
>
> Proletariat
>
> Schlieffen Plan
>
> Anomie
>
> Berlin Congress (1885)

Note that this example allows you to choose five items from a list of eleven. Sometimes, however, you will not be given this much choice. In the present case, it probably will not help you to answer more than five.

Once you have determined which five terms you understand best, you must undertake two operations: "identify" and "explain the significance." To identify, you need to demonstrate that you know who or what the item is. If you chose the first item, for example, you might begin: "Eiffel Tower—A large metal tower designed by the engineer Eiffel and constructed as part of the 1889 World's Fair in Paris." This explains what the Eiffel Tower is, situates it in time, gives its location, and even specifies its designer. In this single sentence, you have demonstrated that you know something about the building beyond the fact that it often appears on posters.

After you have identified the item, you still need to explain its significance. You must state why the item is important in relation to the themes of the course. For instance, in a course on the history of architecture, the significance of the Eiffel Tower might have to do with how it was actually constructed or with the relationship between its design and the styles of the period.

You should also think about how an item fits into the scheme of the course. Thus, in a course on "Social Trends of Post-Enlightenment Europe," your answer might be as follows:

> *Eiffel Tower—A large metal tower designed by the engineer Eiffel and constructed as part of the 1889 World's Fair in Paris. Created to illustrate the new technologies, it was rejected by traditionalists, but it rapidly became a symbol of the belief in progress of the late nineteenth century and was soon associated with the French avant garde.*

This answer clearly identifies the phenomenon and explains its significance in terms of economic, social, and intellectual trends. Relating the item to the main aspects of the course demonstrates that you can connect specific details to the broader themes.

■

PERSONAL LEARNING QUESTION

How would you go about describing to someone the difference between the word *identify* and the word *explain*?

■

ESSAY QUESTIONS

Essay questions require the skills required for multiple-choice and short-answer identification and more. As with multiple-choice questions, it is necessary to read the question carefully so that you know exactly what is being asked. Like identification questions, essay questions involve relating specific details to the broader themes in the course. In addition, writing skills are involved.

The essay is a coherent explanation of concepts that are supported by details and that also responds to distinctive issues raised in the course. You, not the instructor, will have to establish the general context for the material. To help you devise an effective strategy, we will examine each of the operations needed for writing essays.

Essay Exams: The Nine Basic Instructions

The first step in writing an essay is to make sure that you understand what is meant by the words in the question. Pay special attention to the words directing you, because they carry the clues to what the instructor actually expects in your answer. The following are common directives:

Compare

Contrast

Compare *and* Contrast

Define

Discuss

Enumerate

Evaluate

Explain

Show

Compare means to show the similarities between two things, such as events, periods, or people. For instance, if the question reads, "Compare the strategies of Alexander the Great and Augustus for establishing the legitimacy of their rule," you are expected to discuss the similarities between the leadership styles of these two leaders. Take note: instructors are not always precise in their terminology. The term compare is used broadly with the expectation that a student will contrast differences (see below), or evaluate the similarities. Therefore, if in doubt, you may be wise to discuss some differences and draw some conclusions between the two items.

Contrast, on the other hand, means to find differences. If you were asked to "Contrast the image of the ideal man with that of the ideal woman in Victorian culture," you would focus on the differences between the two. You might begin by discussing the notion of what Victorian women were supposed to be like, move on to ideas about the men, and then point out the differences. Or, you could move back and forth between details on each side.

A common instruction on essay exams is to *compare and contrast,* calling for both the similarities and the differences. If you were asked to compare and contrast the French and the American Revolutions, it might help to quickly list things alike and different on scratch paper. You then could organize your essay either to discuss the similarities and differences in sequence or to move back and forth between revolutions.

When an essay question asks you to *define* a term or phrase, first indicate which group of things it belongs to. For example, if given the term "the Hague," begin your definition by saying "The Hague is a city . . . ," followed by its differences from other cities and at least one specific example. (See the section on short-answer questions for a fuller discussion of how to define a concept.) Complete definitions often form the core of an essay.

Describe means to give a full picture of the subject by providing examples and elaborating on its characteristics. The difference between "define" and "describe" is subtle. While much of the content of one answer would also appear in the other, the word *describe* implies a report built around examples, whereas *define* emphasizes a profile of a topic.

Discuss usually means to explore a topic from various points of view, perhaps giving pros and cons. For instance, in answer to the question, "Discuss the causes of the First World War," you would first present several factors that may have led to the outbreak of war and then discuss the validity of each. When discussing, offer specific evidence to support or undercut each possible explanation, possibly mentioning historians or schools of thought that have defended each factor.

Enumerate essentially means to make a list. This instruction suggests that the professor wants a streamlined answer rather than a discussion of various viewpoints. However, enumerating means more than simple listing or outlining. If you encountered the question "Enumerate the reasons many American colonists chose to revolt against England," for example, you should begin by making a list of major factors (taxation, ideas of representative government, arbitrary actions by the English government, etc.). Then, strengthen the list by describing and evaluating the importance of each factor.

Evaluate means to make a judgment or take a stand. Teachers sometimes will expect you to evaluate a position by asking you to agree or disagree with that position. In the following example, notice how the question asks for response to a quotation, giving you the opportunity to display your knowledge of the subject. Supported by evidence, your answer should judge the validity of the given statement.

A prominent nineteenth-century British writer claimed that "No empire in history has ever been built on nobler motives than our own." Evaluate this statement in terms of what you have learned about the expansion of the British Empire in Asia in the eighteenth and nineteenth centuries.

If you chose to refute this claim of noble motives, you could point to the Opium Wars. Contrary to acting nobly, British warships forced the Chinese to accept opium from India despite the fact that it was destroying the moral fiber of Chinese society. You should use a series of examples to support the position you have taken in response to the quotation.

Explain means to interpret a given generalization by using specific facts and ideas. If the question asks you to explain how industrialization undermined the position of the European aristocracy in the nineteenth century, your answer will accept, rather than refute, the given statement and work from that assumption. However, often you may also mention counterexamples and thus show a fairly complex understanding of an issue.

If asked to *show* the truth of a statement or the reasons for a historical event, your answer should be more of an explanation than a judgment. Consider the following question: "Show how the conditions of colonial life created problems that have continued to plague Latin America ever since the wars of independence." Acceptance of the claim that the legacy of colonial rule created problems is a given. Therefore, your task will be to enumerate the problems created in the colonial period, explain why they came into being, and analyze how they have affected the region since independence.

Understanding these nine key instructions can help you effectively convey your knowledge of the subject. However, bear in mind that not all teachers use these terms in precisely the same way. Become experienced with the wording of essay questions by reading exams from a variety of history courses. This experience will help you anticipate what the instructor expects in your answer.

∎

PERSONAL LEARNING QUESTION

Exactly what are you expected to do when you are presented with an exam question that contains the following terms: "compare," "contrast," "compare and contrast," "define," "discuss," "enumerate," "evaluate," "explain," or "show."

∎

Understanding the Directions in Essay Questions

Essay questions can be very complex. If you read a question carefully, you will usually see a cluster of embedded questions that need to be sorted out. For example, an American history exam might contain a question like the following:

> *Discuss the common features of the major utopian communities in the nineteenth century and the distinguishing philosophy of each.*

This question actually contains four directions: (1) define **utopian communities** in the nineteenth century, (2) decide which of these communities were significant, (3) describe their common features, and (4) compare their philosophies.

When attacking a complex question, stop to consider what the question requires before you begin writing or you may miss an essential part. Pay close attention to the wording. Here are some pitfalls to watch for.

1. Don't fail to notice the time frame. This question specifies "nineteenth century," so avoid wasting time describing earlier or more recent utopian communities.

2. Formulate a usable definition. In this instance, defining "utopian communities" helps you eliminate some groups and focus on ones that fit your definition.

3. Look for qualifiers. The word "major" in our example suggests that the essay should describe only the most important utopian communities. This instructor is looking for depth, not quantity.

4. Recognize wording that separates ideas. For instance, communities' "features" contrasted with their "philosophies" implies lifestyle versus beliefs.

5. Respond to the whole question. The words "common features" could lead you to write the entire essay on the similarities of these societies, unless you notice the phrase "philosophy of each," which demands individual treatment as well. Conversely, don't focus entirely on the philosophies and leave out the communities' common aspects.

Restating the Question

Rather then trying to second-guess a complex essay question, just restate it at the beginning of your essay. Restating the question as you understand it has two advantages. For one thing, it forces you to understand the question. Second, it allows the instructor to see your intentions. Addressing the parts of a complex question gives you a starting point and organization for the rest of the essay.

If the question itself is wordy and confusing, restating it helps you get to the core of the question. Look at this wordy version of our last example.

> *While they were often attacked, the communes of the 1960s looked back to a long tradition of utopian communities in America. Like abolitionism, temperance, and women's suffrage, these movements captured the moral fervor of the times. Some, like the Oneida community, survived for decades. Others, like Owen's New Harmony community, disappeared in a matter of months. Discuss the more important of these communities and their philosophies.*

This version is ambiguous. Does the instructor intend for you to compare the nineteenth and twentieth centuries' utopian communities, or is the first part just an introduction? What about the references to abolitionism, temperance, and women's suffrage? Are they just background or are they intended as part of the answer? Should you concentrate exclusively on the Oneida community and New Harmony?

When faced with a confusing question like this, you sometimes can ask the instructor for clarification at the beginning of the exam. Beyond that, the best thing to do is to restate the question the way you intend to answer it. The smartest way to handle an ambiguous essay question is to refine the question but also refer to the things mentioned in the original question. By doing this, you focus on the core and still cover yourself in case the other stuff was important to the instructor.

To answer our example question, you could zoom in on the nineteenth-century utopian communities, describing their lifestyles and contrasting their philosophies. Include the Oneida community and New Harmony. At the end, compare your essential points about these societies with the modern movements mentioned in the question.

To speed up this process, prepare for an essay exam by reading a wide range of essay questions. Take them apart and think about how to answer them. Learn to distinguish the crucial subject matter from background material. When you read an essay question, be sure to recognize the time frame and qualifiers.

Organizing an Essay

Some essay questions actually spell out how the instructor expects your essay to be organized. Examine the following essay question, for example.

> *Choose one of the essays listed below and do the following: (1) give the essay an approximate date, (2) summarize its major argument(s), and (3) discuss its significance for broader themes in American intellectual life from the same period.*

> *a) Charlotte Perkins Gilman, selection from* Women and Economics

> *b) Jane Addams, "The Subjective Necessity of Social Settlements"*

> *c) John Dewey, selection from* The Public and Its Problems

> *d) Randolf Bourne, "Trans-national America"*

After selecting the topic with which you feel most comfortable, just use the outline given by the question. The three steps in this sample question create an outline that progresses from factual information about the literature to an analysis of how the literature fits into history. The question organizes your essay to move toward more complex reasoning, the kind of reasoning most valued in a course on history.

In many cases, however, you will be responsible for deciding how to organize your essay. In the following section, we will offer a complete procedure for organizing your essay. Remember, though, you have to be flexible. Adapt this procedure to your own learning style, the nature of the question, and the time constraints of the examination.

Outlining an Essay

First, read the question carefully and decide what it calls for. As you break up the question to understand it, use the embedded directions to organize your ideas. Apply your knowledge of the course to each embedded question and consider how all the questions connect with each other. Then, using only a few key words, make a brief outline to put the topics in the order you want in the essay.

Devoting a couple of minutes to organization at the beginning of the exam period can have a major impact on what you write down later. Your outline will guide your thinking and keep you from getting off track. To illustrate how using a short outline works, here is an example from a European history course.

Discuss the dynamics of European empire building from the advent of the "new imperialism" to the onset of World War I. What were the consequences of imperialism for both European powers and colonial peoples?

First, take the question apart to see the embedded directions. In this example, there are five of them: (1) describe how Europe built its empires during this period, (2) define and explain the significance of "new imperialism," (3) indicate why this era ended when World War I began, (4) describe the consequences of imperialism for European peoples, and (5) describe the consequences of imperialism for colonial peoples.

To save time, write this list in your own shorthand. Scale back phrases and abbreviate as many words as will still be intelligible. For example, (1) Descr. Emp. Build., (2) Def. New Imper., and so on. Think of ideas or details from the readings, lectures, and discussion that answer each step. As you have learned, studying systematically not only plants the concepts in your mind, but also files them so you can retrieve the appropriate answers to these questions.

Now that you have a series of topics ready to write out, decide how you want to arrange them. You could follow the order in which you wrote the questions (1–2–3–4–5), or you might begin with World War I, the end of this era, and describe the developments that led up to it (3–1–2–4–5). Organize the topics to flow from one to another, remembering to include a short introduction and conclusion. Then, assign a certain number of minutes to each section and begin writing.

A hint: lay out your best part early on so you do not get caught in a time crunch at the end of the exam period. If you do run out of time before finishing your essay, copy the rest of your preparation outline into the exam booklet. A rough outline is no substitute for a well developed essay, but it will demonstrate that you have more ideas.

Some essay questions provide very few organizational guidelines. Suppose, for instance, the question asks you to discuss how the concept of the artist's relationship to society changed over the entire period of the course. It is up to you to produce names of artists, descriptions of their art, the relation of the art to their society, and society's changing attitude towards its artists. In effect, you have to provide all the content and create your own structure. Preparatory outlining is especially valuable for loose essay questions, because topics develop around the minor questions you choose to ask.

This strategy will guide you even if you're hit with the ultimate open-ended essay question. For example,

Write a question that embraces what you think have been the major themes in this course. Answer it.

To answer this, you must determine what the main themes of the course are, then use them to create a question and organize your answer. If you are already used to organizing information around questions you pose, this one might even be fun.

■

PERSONAL LEARNING QUESTIONS

How would you rate your outlining abilities? What would you change to become more effective in organizing answers to essay questions?

■

Hypothetical Questions

All the essay questions we have considered thus far ask students to interpret historical situations they have actually studied. Let us now consider exam questions that ask you to use your reasoning powers and knowledge of the course material to analyze issues *not* covered in class. Does this sound crazy?

If you thought that the instructor is testing to see *how much you know,* you may be surprised to learn that he or she really is interested in *how well you understand and apply* history. When you are asked **hypothetical questions,** you must draw on your knowledge of the subject to make comparisons to the unknown. If you feel uncomfortable with what seems like guessing, remember that the point of this type of question is to reveal your ability to interpret and make active use of what have learned.

One way to get you to apply what you know is for the question to present new information and ask you to analyze it based on something you have studied. In the following example, imagine that your African American history class has been studying *Blues People,* by LeRoi Jones.

*One distinguishing feature of the culture of the 1930s was the cel-
ebration of folk cultures by mostly urban, middle-class Americans.
Artists, intellectuals, and reformers sought to document folk cultures and even tried deliberately to create them. How would you
compare those efforts to the tradition of black folk culture LeRoi
Jones describes in* Blues People? *How do you think Jones would
view the celebration of folk culture by white Americans in the
1930s?*

Because the statements about the 1930s celebration of folk cultures are
given information, you will not be expected to elaborate on them. Accept the statements and concentrate on LeRoi Jones. You are being
asked to imagine what LeRoi Jones would have to say about the white
middle-class interest in folk culture. Your interpretation will reveal how
well you understand Jones's attitudes and ideas. Compare and contrast
what you learned about black folk culture through reading *Blues People* to the statement given in the question. Only a thorough understanding of Jones's book will enable you to respond effectively to this
question.

Kevin's Experience with Historical Science Fiction   Kevin misunder-
stood the purpose of this hypothetical exam question.

*It is the year 2025, and human civilization as we know it is in cri-
sis. You have been selected to enter a time machine and return to
the nineteenth century to bring back representatives from three
utopian communities to advise world leaders on how to structure
human society for survival. Discuss the features of the three communities you would choose, the philosophy of each, and how you
believe they could contribute to the survival of human society.*

Searching his memory, Kevin could not recall hearing or reading anything that connected the utopian communities of the nineteenth century to problems in the future. How could he even know for sure what
the problems of the future might be? How was he supposed to answer
such a question? Either his memory was failing him or the instructor
was asking a question that wasn't fair. He wrote down a few things
about nineteenth-century utopian societies and went on. He received
only three out of a possible ten points on that question.

When Kevin spoke with several friends after the exam, he found
that no one had gotten more than five points on that question. So, he
and a couple of other students went to the instructor's office to complain. They pointed out that the question asked for material that hadn't

been presented. Obviously, no one could answer the question adequately. This class, they angrily insisted, was supposed to be about history, not science fiction. The instructor listened to the students' complaints, but she replied that the question was a fair way to assess students' understanding of the material on nineteenth-century utopian societies. She had presented it in a *problem-solving format* because she expected students to be able to use what they had learned in a new situation, not just recall and regurgitate what had been presented in class.

The fact that 2025 had not arrived was irrelevant. The essence of the question—and the basis for grading—concerned how nineteenth-century utopians went about resolving human problems. Students could have focused on any major world problem that might still be present in 2025: world peace, environmental concerns, or economic growth, for example. The important thing was the student's description of how nineteenth-century utopians would handle that problem.

You may not like hypothetical questions, but it is a fact of life that teachers use them. Therefore, you should recognize why these questions are asked and how you can respond to them. In this case, Kevin's teacher wanted students to think critically, draw inferences and connections, and extend their knowledge into arguments and problem solving. She believed that having knowledge means being able to use it for thinking and reasoning. She was convinced that a student who really understands the philosophies and operations of nineteenth-century utopian societies should be able to apply that understanding to human relationships today and in the future.

It is ironic that Kevin knew enough about nineteenth-century utopian communities to make an "A" on the more straightforward version of this question presented earlier in this chapter. He knew the basic ideas of the utopians and could have applied them if he had been aware of the reasons why hypothetical essay questions are asked.

Relating History to Current Events   Many hypothetical questions ask you to relate historical knowledge to events closer at hand. Here is an example: Can the revolutions in East-Central Europe and the former Soviet Union be thought of as another form of decolonization, comparable to the postwar decline of West European imperialism? How do the problems of the new nations in East-Central Europe compare to those of nations in decolonized Africa and Asia?

At the heart of a question like this is the notion of comparison. It expects you to see the *analogy* between one situation and another. Analogical reasoning forms the basis of a great deal of learning. When you face a new situation, such as starting a new job, you bring knowledge gained from previous work experiences. Knowledge of history operates the same way. If you really understand the process of decolonization following World War II, you should be able to use that knowledge to analyze more recent events.

Be aware that historical parallels are always potentially risky. The trends of one period do not necessarily apply to another time. Therefore, some essay exams will ask you to judge whether or not it is reasonable to compare the two situations. An exam on twentieth-century American history, for example, might include the following question.

> *In the months before the Persian Gulf War, President Bush argued that Saddam Hussein was another Hitler and implied that failure to go to war with him would be a return to the appeasement policy of the 1930s. Others argued that the situation more closely resembled that at the beginning of the war in Vietnam and that the beginning of hostilities would lead the United States into a costly and interminable war.*
>
> *Evaluate the use of these comparisons of the American situation in the fall of 1990 with those of the late 1930s and the middle 1960s. To what extent (if any) were these parallels justified historically?*

The question is not asking you to debate the wisdom of American involvement in the Persian Gulf War, but rather to evaluate the comparisons to former wars. Your answer first would discuss how each side used historical analogies to support their opinions about the Persian Gulf War. Then, based on your knowledge of American foreign policy in the 1930s and 1960s, you would evaluate the claims. You would determine which historical situation offers the better comparison to these current events. Your essay will show how well you can use what you have learned to analyze events as they happen.

■

PERSONAL LEARNING QUESTIONS

Are you intimidated by hypothetical questions? Why or why not?

■

OTHER TYPES OF EXAMS

Take-Home Exams

Up to now, we have concentrated on in-class exams, since they are by far the most common. Some courses, however, will give you the opportunity to work on an essay outside the confines of a testing period. Taking home an exam has its advantages, for you will have more time to think about the question and organize your ideas. On the other hand, the instructor will expect a more polished answer.

Take-home exams combine the elements of an in-class exam and a paper. Even if you're given a couple of days to complete and turn in the exam, you should begin studying in advance, as you would for an in-class exam. You need to already have the concepts in the forefront of your mind so that your answer will have a chance to evolve. Use our chapter on writing papers to develop a take-home exam that is well written. The techniques described there will help you improve your essay through planning and rewriting.

Open-Book Exams

Open-book exams allow you to use your notes and texts during the exam. If you think this will make things easier, don't get too excited, because you must be well prepared for this kind of test. Questions on an open-book exam usually are complex. You will need to have your information sources organized so that you can conveniently pull out the facts you need to build a cogent essay. You definitely will not have time to reread a semester's lecture notes from scratch. The best thing you can bring to an open-book exam is your own fully developed, systematized study guide.

What Can You Take for Granted?

All writing is directed at a particular audience, but there is something unusual about the audience of essay exams. Normally, someone who knows something very well explains it to someone who knows it less well. The explainer must clarify anything that the other person does not understand. In an exam situation, however, the roles are reversed. You will be explaining something to someone who (presumably) knows it better. What do you have to spell out and what can you take for granted?

The answer to this question can have a great effect on your grade. If you fail to explain something important, your grader may assume that you do not know it. If, on the other hand, you spend a great deal of time explaining the obvious, you will have less time to develop and support your argument.

There are no fixed rules that you can apply to all situations. In general, however, you do not have to explain anything that it is reasonable to assume any educated person would know. For example, if you were writing about the Boston Tea Party for an American history exam, you probably would not be expected to explain that Boston is in Massachusetts and that Massachusetts formerly was an English colony on the eastern coast of North America. By contrast, it might be important to explain that the Boston Tea Party was an example of the alliance between wealthy New England merchants and the poorer classes in the city. This is not general knowledge and, if it were relevant to the question and did not appear, your instructor might think that you had not learned the material.

APPLICATION EXERCISES

1. Plan a study guide for your history course making use of organizational strategies that work for you. Following are some decisions to consider.

    What will be the overall form of your guide?

    Looseleaf notebook divided into sections
    File folders in a box
    Set of spiral notebooks
    Looseleaf notebook + computer files
    File box + computer files
    Spiral notebooks + computer files
    Other _____

    How will the guide be organized?

    By major topics in the course
    By activities (reading, lectures, discussion, exams, etc.)
    By dates (daily, weekly, biweekly)
    Other _____

    How will you use the guide?

    To organize and synthesize material
    To review material regularly
    To use in discussion with others
    To prepare for exams
    Other _____

2. Find out what you can about the examinations given by your history instructor. Following are possible sources of this information.

   The instructor of the course

   The discussion leader of the course

   Public test files in the campus library or elsewhere

   Students who have already taken the course from this instructor

   Your own previous tests

   When you have this information, make up questions in each format from the material assigned for your next exam. Answer these questions to practice organization, recall, and efficiency. Use the questions and their answers in discussion and study sessions with other students in the class.

3. Obtain an old examination from the history course you are now taking (by the same instructor) or ask the instructor to provide the class with samples of the kinds of questions to be included on the next exam. Then, analyze this exam or set of sample questions to determine the ways in which you'll be expected to respond. Use the following checklist as a guide.

   Does the examination include multiple-choice questions? If so, determine which of the following kinds of multiple-choice questions are represented:

   ____ Simple recall

   ____ Interpretive

   ____ Application or problem solving

   ____ Other _____

   Does the examination include short-answer questions? If so, determine which kinds of short answers are required:

   ____ Specific items such as names and dates

   ____ Complex items such as definitions and explanations

   ____ Other _____

   Does the examination include quick recognition items such as true-false, matching, and/or identification? If so, determine whether these items deal with particular facts, concepts, and/or arguments.

   Does the examination include essay questions? If so, determine which of the following categories these questions might fall into:

_____ Simple (one basic question)

_____ Complex (two or more interrelated questions as subparts of the main question)

_____ Going beyond material presented in class and readings

_____ Problem solving

_____ Other _____

What percentage of a test is likely to be devoted to each type of question?

Is a test cumulative (covers all material up to that point in the semester) or limited (to material covered since the last test)?

4. Identify the kinds of test questions you have most trouble with that are also included in your instructor's tests. Plan a strategy for improving your success with these kinds of items.

TERMS TO KNOW

essay questions

exam performance strategies

exam preparation strategies

hypothetical questions

interpretive multiple-choice items

recall multiple-choice items

short-answer questions

study guide

super map

utopian community

CHAPTER 8

WRITING PAPERS

- *What are the parts of a good history paper and how can you best put them together?*

- *How can you formulate a question around which to build a history paper?*

- *How can you know if your paper is too big or too small?*

- *How can you lead your reader through your paper smoothly?*

- *How can you use rewriting to strengthen your paper?*

- *How can you avoid plagiarism?*

- *How can you find primary and secondary sources for your paper?*

Throughout this book, we have suggested that you will be more successful in history courses if you learn to perform like a historian. Whether you are writing a short-answer essay or a senior thesis, as soon as you begin to combine writing and thinking about the past, you *become* a historian.

Your history course prepares you for this step. You listen to lectures, read textbooks and primary sources, participate in discussion, and prepare for and take exams. You learn to read and listen critically, to isolate clues relevant to the problem at hand, and to form interpretations and support them. These skills prepare you for writing a research paper.

Even if you don't plan to become a historian, writing a history paper is good preparation for any professional career. You will be expected to take in information, separate what is relevant and reliable from what is not, create an interpretation based on this evidence, develop a systematic defense for your position, and communicate your ideas in a coherent manner. Whether you are preparing a business report, researching a problem, or applying for a grant, you need these skills.

BASIC COMPONENTS OF A HISTORY PAPER

History papers usually include the following elements:

- A question or issue
- An interpretation of the issue stated as a **main thesis**
- An **argument** defending the interpretation
- Evidence that makes the argument plausible
- Consideration of **counterarguments**
- A conclusion that restates the superior value of the author's argument
- A **bibliography** of references

Regardless of the length of your paper, it is wise to include all these components. They do not have to appear in the order given here.

Following is a short paper actually written by a student in a European history course. When the class studied the development of the idea of **progress**, Todd was asked to write a short essay discussing whether or not the late-eighteenth-century French philosopher Condorcet represented a break in Western thinking about history. Watch how smoothly a paper can develop using the component guidelines.

Question or Issue[1]

Condorcet is seen by many as being the father of a break in traditional thinking, specifically with respect to the idea of progress and enlightenment.

Having established the general subject, Todd proceeded to take a position.

Thesis

While it is true on the surface that Condorcet's ideas do differ radically from previous (particularly Christian) thought, closer examination demonstrates that many of Condorcet's ideas are rooted in such thought.

Next, Todd considered the opposite position or counterargument (i.e., that Condorcet's thought was radically different from that which preceded him).

Consideration of Counterarguments

Condorcet's most obvious break with tradition stems from his view of the Church (and Christianity) as a root of evil in society which inhibits mankind from achieving its true potential. Condorcet notes: "We have watched man's reason being slowly formed by the natural progress of civilization; we have watched superstition seize upon it and corrupt it, and tyranny degrade and deaden the minds of men under the burden of misery and fear" (Condorcet, 124).

Condorcet also refutes several ideas of Christian thinking. Traditional Christian thought states that because of original sin and the immoral nature of man, humans can never achieve a perfect world on earth. One of the best examples of this thought is found in

---

[1]The titles of the sections were added for the present discussion and were not part of the original essay.

St. Augustine's The City of God, *in which he notes that the earthly existence was "one of eternal sin and suffering" (Wagar, 57). Furthermore, Condorcet dismisses the Christian concept of faith in favor of the truth and empiricism of the sciences proposed by scholars such as Descartes and Locke (Condorcet, 133, 137). Condorcet holds that through science, in opposition to the faith of* **Scholastics** *such as Aquinas and Bonaventure, man can arrive at truth and reason based on the laws of nature (Condorcet, 132, 133, 136, 148, 194). Condorcet goes a step further and contradicts Christian views by stating that through reason man can achieve morality on earth (Condorcet, 128, 134, 192). Most significantly, Condorcet notes, "The real advantages that should result from this progress, of which we can entertain a hope that is almost a certainty, can have no other term than that of the absolute perfection of the human race."(Condorcet, 184).*

Now, having laid out the general question and the arguments that could be used on the other side, Todd returns to his own position. Superficially, Condorcet's thought may seem to represent a revolution, he tells his readers, but on a deeper level it continues earlier traditions.

Argument Supporting the Paper's Thesis

While on the surface it appears that Condorcet's world departs radically from Christian thought, closer examination shows that his ideas are actually based on Christian thought. One can observe that the very idea of a linear growth or "progress" has its roots in Christianity as opposed to the cyclical beliefs of pre-Christian cultures (Wagar, 55, 56, 60). In Condorcet's world, as in Christianity, humankind does arrive at a state of perfection, the essential difference being that Condorcet's perfection occurs on earth instead of in the afterlife.

In addition, Condorcet does admit that, even though his world is built on science, this science must accept certain "laws of nature" which man must have faith in and may never be able to fully understand (Condorcet, 9, 184, 199). One also recognizes that, like Medieval Christianity, Condorcet's worldview was missionary in nature. Condorcet notes that science "will turn its efforts to distant lands, once there are no longer at home any crass prejudices to combat, any shameful errors to dissipate." (Condorcet, 177)

Todd has argued that his interpretation (Condorcet's thought has much in common with earlier Christian ideas) is deeper and more convincing than the opposite position, (Condorcet's ideas are a radical break with the Church). Now, he moves on to clinch the argument with a clear statement of his own position supported by the work of historian Carl Becker.

Conclusion Defending the Paper's Argument

Rather than a total break from tradition, Condorcet's world can be seen more as a logical transition for a populace grown weary with a Church that through much of the late Middle Ages appeared to concentrate much more on politics than theology. Brought up with the idea of hope, Condorcet gave people an opportunity to break at least partially with the Church and channel that hope elsewhere (Becker, 12–15).

Notice that Todd supported his argument with specific references to the readings throughout this essay. He referred to specific passages in the writings of Condorcet himself and also to historians Warren Wagar and Carl Becker, who supported opposing positions of the issue. While demonstrating his familiarity with the assigned passages from Condorcet and the secondary readings, Todd has made active use of the material to support his own argument.

Like all research papers, Todd's paper ended with a bibliography, a listing of the sources of his evidence. In a longer research paper, it would have been necessary also to provide complete bibliographical information in footnotes. Because this paper was a short essay based on assigned material, he gave credit to the ideas of others simply by providing the name of the author and the page number in parentheses. He included the following bibliography at the end of the paper so that his reader could look up his references.

Works Cited

Becker, Carl. *"Progress."* The Idea of Progress Since The Renaissance. *New York: Wiley, 1969: 9–18.*

Condorcet. *"Sketch for a Historical Picture of the Human Mind." Condorcet: Selected Writings. (Course packet)*

Wagar, Warren W. *"The Idea of Progress Since the Renaissance."* Journal of the History of Ideas *27 (Jan-Mar 1967): 55–70.*

BUILDING A PAPER

In the previous section, we analyzed a finished paper. Don't assume that organized and well-argued papers just leap automatically out of the brains of gifted writers. Producing a paper is a complex, creative process. In this section, we will identify discrete steps that will help you develop a polished research paper.

Papers, like houses, start with a blueprint. Then, the foundation is laid and the structure framed, with the finishing work smoothing out the rough look. Writing a paper has one important difference, however. The stages of house construction have to come in a specific order. Once a stage is completed, it is quite costly to go back and make changes. With a paper, on the other hand, switching among steps of composition and rearranging material is quite easy, especially if you are working on a computer.

Building a paper = Understand the assignment

+

Gather information

+

Sift through that information to determine what is relevant

+

Play with ideas

+

Define the central problem or issue

+

Create a tentative thesis or argument

+

Search for relevant evidence or arguments to support your position

+

Outline counterarguments and find responses to them

+

Devise a tentative outline or plan

+

Write a draft

+

Reread the draft critically (as if it were written by someone else)

+

Polish the paper until it is ready

Each paper follows a unique path. The process of gathering information, for example, may be relatively brief, or, in the case of a major thesis, it may take months. You might move through the steps in the order given here or you might begin by writing a **draft** off the top of your head, then going back through the earlier steps to turn it into a well-argued essay. Most good writers, in fact, alternate between gathering information and formulating ideas.

Use this list to develop your own strategy for writing papers. Even if you don't use the exact steps given here, you will know when you have omitted an important process, such as defining the issue. At the very least, we hope this guide prevents such disasters as following all the steps except for the first—understanding the assignment.

■

PERSONAL LEARNING QUESTION
Create in your mind a paper topic for the course you are taking. What would the basic elements of this paper look like?

■

Choosing a Topic[2]

Todd's short paper on Condorcet was written in response to a specific question given by the instructor. If you are not provided with a question, you need to formulate one. Remember the IPSO structure discussed earlier in this book: Issue, Position, Support, Outcome. The central question will identify your issue and set up the rest of the paper.

A good central question or issue must be relevant to the material you have been studying and to the instructions given for the assignment. It should raise important and interesting points. If possible, check your topic with the instructor to make sure that it matches his or her expectations. To help get you started phrasing a question, remember that thesis questions usually begin with one of the following:

---

[2]Parts of the following description of the writing process are adapted from Roland Huff and Charles R. Kline, Jr., *The Contemporary Writing Curriculum: Rehearsing, Composing, and Valuing* (New York: Teachers College Press, 1987).

"Why?" "How?" "What were the most important?" "What were the principal differences between?" or "When did this change occur?"

Phrasing the issue in a single question forces you to clarify the content of your paper. The question, "How did Asian peoples respond to European traders?" might seem like a good basis for a paper. Once you started researching, however, you might find that the term "Asian" is broader than you thought. Is the paper about China and Japan, or about India, Southeast Asia, and Korea as well? Is there enough in common about the reactions of these diverse cultures to write a coherent paper? Similarly, the term "European traders" could refer just to nine-teenth-century merchants bearing the products of the Industrial Revolution or it could refer to the entire range of traders from Marco Polo to modern soft drink companies. Even the words "respond to" may be ambiguous. Did you have in mind official government policies toward outside trade, or popular attitudes to foreign traders, or both? The question is, in fact, a whole bundle of questions.

Just putting your issue into words helps focus it. You might, for example, redefine the earlier question to read, "What were the policies of the Chinese and Japanese governments toward foreign trade in the second half of the nineteenth century?" or, "How did Chinese intellectuals view European traders from the thirteenth to the beginning of the nineteenth centuries?" Defining the issue makes your paper coherent and helps you state the position you will support.

Goldilocks and The Three History Questions[3]

You remember the story of Goldilocks: how, at the bear's place, whether she tried the soup, the chairs, or the bed, it was always a matter of finding the one that was neither too big nor too small, but "just right." Choosing a paper topic can work much the same way.

So imagine Goldilocks is taking a course in modern African history, and, because Goldilocks is minoring in comparative litera-ture, she is particularly interested in the ways in which literary works illuminate historical material. The instructor assigns a ten-page paper, and Goldilocks tries to think of a suitable topic.

---

[3]We wish to thank Thomas Prasch for the material used here.

The first idea that springs into her head is to do a survey of African literature written during the period of decolonization. She can think of a variety of ways in which to put the question. How do African writers respond to the changing political climate of the decolonization period? What does the literature of decolonization say about the European imperialist regimes of the previous decades? Do African writers discuss the role of independence movements, colonial elites, and emerging social classes? She even goes to the library and finds a shelf full of African novels from the period. Finally, however, she remembers she is writing ten pages, not a book. "Too big," she concludes.

Next, she thinks of something she saw while digging around in the library: an essay by Chinua Achebe, whose novel Things Fall Apart *she knows was important to the development of modern African literature. The essay was a discussion of Joseph Conrad and the problems Achebe saw in his novel* Heart of Darkness. *Again she started to formulate questions: Why doesn't Achebe like Conrad's novel? Is Achebe's critique a fair indictment of Conrad? At first she becomes excited by the topic, particularly because she has read* Heart of Darkness *in one of her literature classes, and she is very interested in the fact that this African writer found Conrad's criticisms of imperialism inadequate. But then she tries to imagine stretching the answer to this question to ten pages, and she also recognizes that it would be difficult to use very much of what she has learned about the history of Africa into such a topic. "Too small," she decides.*

But, since she does like Achebe, she starts playing around with the idea of using both the essay and the novel Things Fall Apart. *She realizes that she can focus her paper around the question: How did Chinua Achebe view European imperialism and European explanations of imperialism? This central question immediately suggests others that she develop as time and space allow. If his essay about Conrad can be taken as a critique of European approaches to the subject of imperialism, how does Achebe's own novel provide an alternative view? Does Achebe's own account of the new African nations reflect in any way the failures he perceives in the accounts of even those Europeans like Conrad who were critical of imperialism? She immediately sees that she can strengthen the foundations of the paper by looking at other works by or about Achebe as time and space allow. Now she has a question that fits the task at hand.*

"Just right," Goldilocks concludes. And it was.

■

PERSONAL LEARNING QUESTIONS

Think once again of your imaginary paper. What question does it answer? Is there anything ambiguous or vague about the wording of this question? Is there a way to make it more precise? Is your paper topic too big, too small, or just right? What tells you that a paper is too big or too small?

■

Freewriting, Brainstorming, and Predrafting

Don't tense up as you begin working on a paper. Try to allow your thoughts to flow freely. You can start by **freewriting,** recording in a journal your ideas on the topic about which you are going to write. Or, you can try **brainstorming** ideas with someone else in the course. Don't be too critical yet. Just collect thoughts to use more systematically later.

Eventually, brainstorming can evolve into **predrafting.** Just think of an issue or event you want to deal with and start writing. You are not yet writing the paper itself, so you don't need to monitor your writing. Don't worry about references, grammar, or style. Write until you run out of steam, and then start predrafting from a new starting point or go back to gathering information. You will use some of this writing in the final paper and discard some, but for now you are just gathering material with which to work.

Predrafting can be extremely important. Students often are so insecure about research papers that they postpone beginning to write, thinking they have to keep gathering information. When they finally get around to writing, they often discover that they have collected too much material about some topics and not enough about others. You can avoid this problem by going back and forth between research and predrafting.

Formulating a Thesis

By the time you have collected most of your data, refined your central question, and allowed your ideas to develop through freewriting, brainstorming, and predrafting, you will be ready to formulate a position or thesis. This thesis statement generally is an answer to your issue question. Say, for example, you have defined the question, "How did social conditions in Europe in the late nineteenth century lay the foundation for the avant garde in the arts?" Your reading, brainstorming, and predrafting may lead you to this thesis: "The growth in the number of people consuming art, the creation of new media that publicized the work of artists, and the existence of artistic communities in the major cities of Europe allowed artists to explore creative possibilities that would have been strongly discouraged in earlier times."

This thesis may seem long and complex, but it sets up major areas of support for you in the development of your paper. A thesis should be focused enough to produce a coherent paper without raising too many points for the length of your paper. Therefore, a thesis with clear components will guide your research. Also, if you find early on that a topic is unworkable, you will still have time to reshape the issue or rethink the thesis.

Writing a "Treatment"

Hollywood producers, with millions of dollars at stake, require writers to produce "treatments" of proposed movie plots. These short sketches of the film plot enable both the writer and the potential producer to see the story in a nutshell. In the same way, you can test the potential of a history paper topic by writing a one-paragraph treatment. Susan, a freshman, wrote the following treatment for a paper on the start of the Atomic Era. Notice the thesis statement at the beginning of the treatment.

Racism, an ever present element of human nature, resulted in the negative presentation of all Japanese in the American media during World War II. Even during the most intense fighting in Europe, most Americans would not make the claim that all Germans were Nazis. Clearly, there were German citizens who disagreed with the Nazis and were fighting only because they had no choice. While some Japanese did show fanatical support of the war, this was not true of all Japanese citizens, let alone Japanese Americans. The Japanese were not viewed as individuals, but as an entire race. The American media built on these beliefs to convince the American public that all Japanese were "murderous little ape-men" whose only goal was the conquest of Asia and the Pacific (Blum, p. 56).

In the sentences that follow the thesis statement, Susan presents the basic topics to be covered in the paper: the contrast in views about

Germans and Japanese, the treatment of the Japanese as a race, and the role of the media in creating these views. The only major element missing from this treatment is a presentation of counterarguments. Some historians have counterargued that the attack on Pearl Harbor was responsible for the strongly negative image of the Japanese. This can be refuted as insufficient to explain why these negative feelings were generalized to Japanese Americans.

Outlining the Paper

After formulating a major issue, a thesis statement, and a treatment, you can experiment with the layout of the paper. Transfer the main arguments from your treatment to headings in your outline, and fill in the outline with supporting details. Here is an outline of another freshman's paper on Allied bombing during World War II.

Thesis: *Contrary to prewar predictions, the use of airpower did not force a quick end to World War II.*

I. Introduction

Counter argument: II. Prewar Predictions

    A. Highly accurate bombing of enemy
    B. Attack without declaration would lead to quick surrender
    C. Heavy bombing of cities would break civilian morale and social structure

Main argument: III. Actual Conduct of World War II

    A. Bombing accuracy lower than predicted
        1. Difficult to destroy war material plants
        2. U.S. used daylight bombing
            a. Slightly better accuracy
            b. More air crew casualties
        3. Could assist victory on the ground but not win the ground war
    B. Strike without declared war did not guarantee victory
        1. Example: Pearl Harbor

          a. Brought U.S. into WW II

          b. Unified country against Japan

       2. Fear of retaliation unsuccessful

  C. No large-scale breakdown of civilian morale

       1. Fragility of civilians overestimated

       2. Civilians wanted revenge and supported war effort

          a. Pearl Harbor

          b. Blitz on London

          c. German V-weapons

             i. No military value

            ii. Used only as "instrument of terror" and as retaliation on Britain

IV. Conclusion

Using your outline as a guide while you write, map the paper from topic to topic and paragraph to paragraph. Although you should be open to new ideas as you write, having an outline will keep you focused on your subject and your paper's organization.

■

PERSONAL LEARNING QUESTIONS

How could you use brainstorming and prewriting to help turn your topic into a paper?
What might be the central thesis of your paper?
Can you write a one-paragraph "treatment" of the paper?
What can an outline add to the process of writing?

■

Drafting the Paper

All your work up to this stage has made sense only to you, and that was enough. Now, however, you are entering the public sphere. You have to make sense to someone else: a reader. Therefore, you must begin to write with that reader in mind.

Treat your readers like guests. Make sure that everything is neat and in place before they arrive. Invite them in with a clear statement of your thesis or a striking quotation or an anecdote at the very beginning of the paper. Guide them from topic to topic as you might take a guest from room to room. Make sure they understand the layout of the entire house and how one room relates to another. Stop for a moment and offer them a clear explanation of difficult points. Point out interesting things along the way. And, for clarity as well as politeness, make sure that you greet your readers with a clear introduction and leave them with a concluding summary.

Remember that your paper must display a solid structure. To guide your reader smoothly through the topic, you must state where your arguments and evidence are and why they are there. You must clarify the purpose of every paragraph. You also must convey a clear sense of why the paragraphs are arranged in a particular order. Providing a clear structure not only helps your reader, it also makes your arguments accessible.

Also offer signposts for the reader. Each paragraph should begin with a topic sentence that indicates what is contained in the paragraph. Such signposts help the reader keep his or her place because they correspond to topics laid out in the introduction. There also should be smooth transitions between paragraphs so that the reader is led by the hand from one to the next. The introduction and conclusion put the entire work into perspective.

From time to time, pull back and give the reader an "aerial view." Remind your audience what they have read, what is coming, and how the point you are making fits into the big picture. Here's some old advise for writers: "Tell 'em what you are going to tell 'em, tell 'em, and tell 'em what you told 'em." When you're being deliberately redundant, try to rephrase your points.

Finally, think about how to make the paper interesting. What "hooks" can you find to grab your reader? How do the issues you are discussing relate to broader concerns your reader may share? Are there any interesting anecdotes that illustrate your arguments? Are there appropriate metaphors that will not only grab the reader's attention but also make your ideas clearer and tie parts of the paper together?

Rethinking and Rewriting the Paper

A paper is never finished, it is just interrupted at some point called the "due date." You can continue to improve the writing through umpteenth drafts. And, new ideas about your topic may pop into your mind the moment you hand in your paper.

Allow your paper to take new shape as you write it. The predrafting, outlining, and treatment are just the scaffolding that you use in the early stages of a writing project. Take them down when it is time to complete the job. This is important to remember because it is easy to become overly attached to what you have produced. That perfect sentence or brilliant idea from the predraft may have no place in the final product. If something doesn't fit, remove it, for no matter how impressive, it will distract the reader from your point.

We cannot emphasize enough the importance of rewriting. First drafts are usually so tied up with your own thought processes that they are not fully intelligible to other people. Remember, you have been thinking about this material for a while and things that are obvious to you might not be so clear to your reader. Like the math professor who skips complex intermediate steps, saying "This is intuitively obvious," skipping explanations leaves the audience behind.

Without rereading, rethinking, and rewriting, you run the risk of failing to spell out the connection between ideas and the supporting evidence. It is difficult to know when your own writing is awkward, so you must make an effort to be objective. Because you are graded on the basis of what you actually communicate—and developing the ability to communicate is one of the major goals of a college education—you have to learn to translate what is in your mind into a form others can understand.

Each time you reread and rewrite a passage, you will see new ways to communicate your ideas. You might see some material that should be moved to another paragraph. Perhaps the order of the paragraphs does not lead the reader smoothly through the paper or perhaps you have not provided clear signposts along the way. You also may notice ways to clarify your ideas. You will begin to see connections you missed in the first draft, new ways to present evidence, or counterarguments to bring up and refute. It is not uncommon for professional historians to discover their most important ideas after they have written a first draft, and you may have the same experience.

There are many ways to increase the effectiveness of rewriting. If you let the paper sit for a day or two, you will be more likely to view it as a person reading it for the first time would. Read your paper aloud to listen for awkward sentences or word choices. Even better, have a friend read it to you. You'll get valuable feedback from someone who is not as familiar with the arguments as you are.

Study groups can provide excellent feedback on papers. Members of a group exchange drafts and give each other advice about what works and what doesn't from a reader's perspective. However, if your feedback is coming from other members of your history class, make sure that this arrangement is acceptable to your instructor. Some teachers think that students should work alone when they are writing papers.

If you are lucky, you will catch the writing bug and begin to enjoy rewriting. Many students come to see the process of writing and rewriting as a form of artistic expression. Let yourself feel the pleasure and sense of mastery as your paper slowly becomes clearer, more insightful, and more elegant in its presentation.

■

PERSONAL LEARNING QUESTIONS
Do you treat your readers like guests when you write a history paper? What would you change about your personal writing style to become a more hospitable host?

■

GIVING CREDIT WHERE CREDIT'S DUE[4]

Putting together a history paper involves research not only in primary sources, but also in writings that deal with related topics. You will refer to ideas or borrow the actual words from other writers, and there is nothing wrong with doing that. However, you *must give credit to those writers,* for both the words and the ideas you borrow from them. Not doing so is **plagiarism.**

In almost any course you take, plagiarism, if detected by the instructor or grader (and you would be surprised how easily most plagiarism is noticed), will guarantee you an F. Furthermore, at most universities, plagiarism can result in disciplinary action, up to suspension or expulsion. It is very important, therefore, to use and cite source material properly.

Here's the basic rule of thumb: if an idea or fact is not your own, and not part of common knowledge, *name your source*. If you use the exact wording of a source, *use quotation marks*. If you're confused about what is or is not common knowledge, remember, *when in doubt,*

---

[4]We wish to thank Thomas Prasch for material in this section.

give a citation. It is always better to cite more than you need to than not as much as you have to.

Most students think of plagiarism only as the blatant copying of entire essays, but even less extensive misuse of sources can get you in trouble. Sometimes, in fact, plagiarism can occur almost unconsciously.

When taking notes on your reading, it is dangerously easy to slip into quotation or partial quotation. Be aware of this danger. The best approach is to use quotations generously in your reading notes, always including quotation marks. Create some note-taking technique that distinguishes between quotation and paraphrase. That way, you'll know when the words are not your own. When you write your paper, check quotations against the source to make sure you copied them right. It helps to list page numbers in your notes.

How Jim Unintentionally Committed Plagiarism

Jim was working on a paper on the development of **nationalism** and national self-consciousness in Argentina. After laying out his introduction, he thought it would be useful to provide a definition of nation. As it happened, one of the books used in his course was Benedict Anderson's *Imagined Communities,* a work that deals with the development of nationalism outside of Europe.

Jim had been impressed with Anderson's definition of nation when he first read it for class. He had summarized Anderson's argument in his reading notes as follows:

Nation = imagined political community, inherently limited and sovereign.

Imagined because the members never know most of their fellow members.

Limited because finite boundaries, beyond which lie other nations.

Sovereign because born in the Enlightenment, destroying the legitimacy of the divinely-ordained dynastic realm.

Community because conceived as deep comradeship.

When writing his paper, Jim dug out his notes, found this passage, and read it over again. He wasn't quite sure what the "sovereign" part meant, but the rest of it sounded clear. He then sat down at his computer and began his next paragraph.

To begin our discussion of Argentinean nationalism I will define what is meant by "nation." A nation is an imagined political community, limited in its character. It is imagined because members of a nation never know most of their fellow members and limited because a nation has finite boundaries. It is a community because it is united by a sense of deep comradeship among its members.

Jim read the passage through and decided it provided exactly the definition he needed. Because he knew the ideas were from Anderson, he threw in a mention of Anderson's book on a "works cited" page at the end of the paper.

Jim was appalled when he got the paper back marked an F. However, he should not have been. Some of the words he used were Benedict Anderson's, not his own. Although he had given credit to Anderson, he had not given enough credit: he had not used quotation marks, even though the words came directly from the book, and he had not indicated a page reference, which suggested to the grader that he was trying to hide what he had borrowed.

Jim made not one but three kinds of mistakes. First, he failed in his note taking. Second, he neither used direct quotations nor paraphrased his source. Third, he didn't even cite his source correctly.

An acceptable use of Anderson's work might look like this.

We should begin our discussion of nationalism by defining what is meant by the idea of "nation." Benedict Anderson has termed nation "an imagined political community ... both inherently limited and sovereign." Nation is "imagined" because it exists in the minds of its members, for, as Anderson points out, "the members of even the smallest nation will never know most of their fellow-members." The idea of nation is "limited" because it is conceived of as having "boundaries, beyond which lie other nations." The idea of sovereignty became linked with that of nation because of the dominant political ideals of the particular period in which the idea of nation was shaped, during the age of the Enlightenment. Finally, Anderson argues, nation is a "community" because it "is always conceived as a deep, horizontal comradeship."[5] A nation is thus only an idea, but nevertheless one that binds people together into a unity.

[5]Benedict Anderson, *Imagined Communities: Reflections of the Origin and Spread of Nationalism,* Rev. ed. (London: Verso Press, 1991), pp. 6–7.

Notice that Anderson is directly credited in the text, and wherever Anderson's words are used directly they are framed by quotation marks. When words are omitted from a direct quotation, ellipsis dots (". . .") indicate the gaps. This writer, unlike Jim, paraphrases portions, putting Anderson's ideas into his own words. See, for example, the writer's point about sovereignty. When this writer is done quoting, he provides a footnote that lists the source, including page references. Finally, at the conclusion of the passage, the writer summarizes Anderson's basic definition in his own words, a way of telling the reader (and the grader) that he understands the material quoted.

Formats for citations vary somewhat among disciplines, with different disciplines and different instructors having their own preferences. There are two general formats: footnotes or **endnotes** and parenthetical citation. An example of footnoting style can be seen in the example given above; an endnote would look the same but be located at the end of the paper. This writer provides one footnote for the entire passage, which is more convenient than footnoting every single quotation. If the quotations had come from more scattered parts of the book, however, this approach would not be adequate.

Note that each citation should include more than just the author and book title. It should also include the edition of the book, the place of publication, the name of the publisher, and the year of publication. If your footnotes or endnotes do not contain everything, you should add a bibliography at the end of the paper listing complete information for all your sources.

Parenthetical citation involves citing the author, year of publication, and page numbers in parentheses immediately following reference an author's work. Here's an example.

. . . was a "deep, horizontal comradeship" (Anderson, 1991: 6–7).

The full bibliography at the end of the paper would be organized according to works cited in parentheses in the text. For example,

(Anderson, 1991)

Benedict Anderson. *Imagined Communities: Reflections of the Origin and Spread of Nationalism,* Rev. ed. London: Verso, 1991.

Because citation formats vary, check with your instructor to see if she or he has any preferences. If not, use the style with which you feel most comfortable. You probably will find that most history professors don't care *how* you go about citing your sources, *just as long as you do it* and *use a consistent format.*

■

PERSONAL LEARNING QUESTIONS

How might you commit plagiarism without intending to? How could you avoid it?

■

CONDUCTING RESEARCH

Plunging into research can be very enjoyable. You can find great pleasure and excitement reading old newspapers or combing through primary documents. It's thrilling to find that perfect example that illuminates everything you have been trying to describe.

Many of the examples presented earlier assumed that you would be basing your paper on materials assigned in class. This section describes how to operate completely on your own as a historian, collecting your own material. You'll need to look both for primary sources written in the period you are studying and for secondary sources written about the period by contemporary scholars.

All of a sudden, the library looks very large and imposing, and you ask questions like, "How am I going to find relevant materials?" and "What am I going to do with them once I have found them?" The job is made even more intimidating by differences among fields within history. The guides and indexes a European historian may employ to find materials are not likely to be the same as those used by an African historian, for instance.

To illustrate how someone conducts research, we're going to follow a student, Lynn, through the process of creating a research paper. The first step is to formulate a topic. Lynn wants to study the role of fallout shelters in American culture in the 1950s and early 1960s. The topic is relevant to issues discussed in her course on American culture since the Depression, and her instructor has enthusiastically endorsed her choice. A brief survey of the documents has determined that she will not have trouble finding source material. To the contrary, she realizes that she eventually will have to narrow the scope of the paper a bit if she is going to finish before the end of the semester.

Lynn needs more information before she can clarify her thesis question. Therefore, she begins a survey of the secondary literature on the topic. With the help of the reference librarian at her college, she develops a strategy for finding materials. She begins with the library's **subject catalog.** Looking under "Postwar U.S. history" and "Civil Defense," she finds several works on American society in the period, two historical works on civil defense, and three works on civil defense actually written in the 1950s. Lynn wants to make very good use of primary sources, so she is disappointed to find that the library only has one of the works from the 1950s.

Because she has gotten an early start on the paper, however—largely as a result of her careful planning for the class in general—she is able to request the other two books through her college library's interlibrary loan service, and they arrive in plenty of time to be used for her paper.

She begins by skimming through the general works on post-World War II America and notes some of the general issues raised about the society at the time, such as the growth of suburbia, the emphasis on the nuclear family, and social conservatism. She reads the works on civil defense carefully, gaining a general knowledge of government policies and popular attitudes in this period.

Now, it is time to begin to search for primary sources. The three books Lynn already has found will be useful, but they are far from sufficient for a long paper. Therefore, she decides to look at **periodicals,** and reviews the *Readers' Guide to Periodical Literature* for each of the years she wishes to study. She finds almost 30 magazine articles on civil defense, although a check of her library's holdings reveals that only 11 of them are actually available. She reads a few of these articles to get a sense of what was being said in the popular media of the 1950s.

Then, she moves on to the government publications section of the library, where she finds six federal and state pamphlets on civil defense. She considers checking newspaper indexes from the period, but decides that the books, magazine articles, and government pamphlets will give her enough information. When one of her classmates hears about Lynn's topic, he mentions *Atomic Cafe,* a documentary film about American cultural and nuclear issues in the 1940s and 1950s. She rents the film from a local video store, and thus has the opportunity to see actual footage from civil defense films of the period.

Lynn is ready to narrow and formulate her thesis question. She is now convinced that civil defense is too broad a topic, but she needs a good focal point to limit the scope of the paper. She thinks back to the issues raised in the general works on American society in the 1950s and to the patterns in the secondary and primary material on civil defense.

Suddenly, it hits her—the family! The NUCLEAR FAMILY! Historians are fascinated by the changes in the family after the Second World War, and the civil defense materials are filled with assumptions about the family. The very notion of a family fallout shelter assumed that the family could be isolated from the rest of society and even from the extended family of grandparents, aunts, and uncles. The books, magazine

SERENDIPITOUS SEARCHING

There are secrets to locating materials for history papers that supplement your standard trek to the card catalog. While some of these methods seem rather random, in fact there is a logic to them. Often, obscure methods will lead you to works your library's subject catalog may omit. A few of these tactics are mentioned here.

Following the footnote trail: If you have found at least one secondary source covering your subject, see what *that* author has looked at. Read the footnotes and bibliography carefully, looking for things that you may be able to use as well. You don't want to do exactly what the author has done with this material, rather, you want to look at the same sources with your own eyes and your own agenda.

The next-shelf method: Again, if you have found at least one book on your topic, look at what's next to it on the shelf. See what books are on the shelves above and below. Library cataloging systems, no matter what system your library uses, are designed to group books by subject. The next-shelf method uses the cataloging work of the librarians to your advantage.

The who's-reviewed approach: If your subject is one that interests other historians, books about it will be reviewed in the professional journals of the discipline. These reviews give you a sense of the arguments historians are making about a particular subject. They often give you leads on other books on a topic that historians think are significant (and sometimes warnings about books most historians dismiss with contempt). The *American Historical Review,* the official journal of the profession, publishes reviews in all fields of history. More specialized journals in each field also review current publications.

articles, pamphlets, and film are filled with images of what the American family was supposed to be like and how it was supposed to act.

Lynn then determines a time frame for her paper. She begins her paper with 1950, because the new nuclear test by the Soviets late in 1949 created the context within which the 1950s' civil defense movement flourished. The reading Lynn has done indicates that attitudes toward nuclear war changed significantly after the Cuban Missile Crisis in 1962, so she uses that year as an endpoint.

She is now ready to formulate her final question: "What assumptions and values concerning the family were reflected in the literature on civil defense from 1950 to 1962?" She can already see how she will explore various aspects of this question: How were men and women portrayed? What were the "appropriate" roles of mothers and fathers? How were children portrayed? How big was the family supposed to be? What values about family and society were present in these works?

Now it is time to find more secondary sources. The reference librarian directs her to *America: History and Life,* the most complete bibliography in the area. There are other useful bibliographies available, but she has been warned to avoid those that include mostly popular newspaper and magazine articles rather than scholarly articles written by historians in professional journals.

She finds eight articles that she can use, ranging from a study of the role of the school system in the civil defense movement to pieces on images of women and the family in 1950s society. She also finds a reference to Paul Boyer's *By the Bomb's Early Light,* a book-length study of American attitudes to atomic issues from 1945 to 1950. Reading relevant sections of this book allows her to set her topic in perspective and raises some conflicting questions that she can address in her paper.

Lynn is now ready to write a first-rate paper. She has created a clear thesis question that ties in with the kinds of questions professional historians are asking about the period. She has a closely related but diverse body of sources on which to base a paper. Lynn goes through the steps of paper writing described above, and she receives—you got it—an A.

■

PERSONAL LEARNING QUESTIONS

**Are you as familiar as you should be with your college library?
How will becoming more familiar with the library help you to
become a more efficient researcher?**

■

WHERE TO LOOK NOW

Many students think that once they've checked the card catalog, their research is done. If the subject is important, they seem to think, there would be a book on it, and the book would necessarily be in the library of their college. Actually, there are far more history books published every year than any library can afford to purchase. And a search of even the largest card catalog will not tell you anything about the journal articles written on a particular topic. Therefore, you will need to broaden your search.

If your library has these guides, the best place to start is with *American History and Life* for topics to do with U.S. history and *Historical Abstracts* for all other fields. These indexes will provide references to almost all the books, articles, and dissertations on virtually any topic in history published in a specific period. If your library does not have these volumes, try the *Humanities Index* and the *Social Science Index,* both of which contain references to historical articles. You will probably wish to ask a reference librarian for help in using these indexes. Check the footnotes and bibliography of the books and articles you have already found to see if they give you other leads. If you find that your library does not have a book or article that you have found a reference to, ask about the possibility of obtaining it through interlibrary loan.

APPLICATION EXERCISES

1. Write a paragraph describing a history paper that you might write for the history course that you are taking. Make sure that you pose a clear and coherent question and indicate what issues will be covered.

2. Ask yourself the following questions about the paragraph you just wrote:

   • Is the question sufficiently precise? Are there vague or ambiguous terms in it?

   • Have I included all the basic elements of a paper except for the bibliography?

   • Is the topic either too big or two small for me to produce a good paper within a semester?

3. Write a plan of research in which you indicate how you would find the sources needed to write this paper.

4. Write a plan in which you describe the steps you would undergo to produce the paper.

5. Find a secondary source that would be useful for this paper. Then, prepare the following:

   - A sentence for the paper in which you quote directly from this source

   - A sentence for the paper in which you use material from this source without quoting

   - Footnotes for each of these sentences

   - A sentence on the same general topic that is based on your general knowledge and that does not require a citation of the author

TERMS TO KNOW

argument
bibliography
brainstorming
counterargument
draft
endnote
footnote
freewriting
main thesis
nationalism
periodical
plagiarism
predrafting
progress
Scholastic
subject catalog

GLOSSARY

analytical reading active reading during which you identify the structure or component parts of a passage. Frequently, analytical reading involves distinguishing between main ideas and supporting ideas or details.

annotating strategically marking a textbook and writing notes in margins during analytical reading so that the textbook becomes a study document.

antebellum the period of American history that came before the Civil War (i.e., before 1860).

argument a principal form of presentation taken in expository writing. An argument includes an issue, a position, evidence, and a conclusion or outcome.

aristrocrats members of the noble class or aristocracy who owed their wealth and status to their ownership of land and to the aristocratic title they inherited from their ancestors (e.g., earl or duke).

assumptions behind every statement there lies certain assumptions or unproven beliefs. Historians are concerned about two types of assumptions. First, they wish to know what people in a particular period took for granted. They ask themselves what did these historical figures believe was so obvious that they did not need to argue about it. Second, historians are interested in the assumptions made by other historians or students of history. In developing an interpretation, one must make certain assumptions about how humans operate or about the reliability of certain pieces of evidence. When historians evaluate an interpretation by another historian or by a student, they consider whether its author made only reasonable assumptions. (See also interpretations.)

bibliography a list of references cited in a paper, presented at the end of the paper so that readers may consult the works used in the preparation of the paper.

biorhythm patterns   your physical pattern of "up" times and "down" times in a 24-hour period. By assessing when you are most alert and when you are least energetic, you can determine your best study times, especially for subjects that demand a lot of concentration and energy.

bourgeoisie   members of the upper middle class. They made their money from commerce, investments, and the professions. Although this social class had been visible earlier in many times and places, it became a particularly important class after the Industrial Revolution. (See also social class and Industrial Revolution.)

brainstorming   talking with others at an early stage in the composition process, putting your thoughts and ideas into words, and getting feedback as you formulate your thesis and plan.

circa   a Latin word meaning "about" or "approximately." It is abbreviated "c," and is used with dates when a historian is not certain exactly when something happened.

collaborative note taking   working with a small group to share notes after each lecture and take turns producing a "master set."

Confucianism   a school of ethics in traditional Chinese society based on the teachings of Confucius (551–479 B.C.). It provided a way of behaving toward other members of society that functioned much like a religion. (See also circa and Taoism.)

contemporary   the most recent period of history, i.e., that which is still in the memory of the living period.

counterarguments   arguments that can be presented against a particular interpretation. It is possible to show that there is evidence that contradicts the original argument, that the main argument is logically contradictory, or that it rests on unreasonable assumptions. (See also interpretations and assumptions.)

cubism   a school of painting in the early twentieth century that broke down visual images into planes and then reassembled them.

cultural history   the study of artistic activity in the past. It may focus on great artists or on broader artistic movements.

culture   in history, as in many other fields, the word culture is used in two different senses. Sometimes it refers to various forms of artistic activity. Other times it is used to describe the customs and beliefs that shape the lives of the members of a particular society. The context in which the term occurs will generally make it clear which is meant.

diplomatic history   the study of the relationship among nations in the past. Traditionally, this included such topics as the strategies of national leaders and treaties. Increasingly, diplomatic history includes the ways in which leaders use foreign policy to increase their power at home.

displacement activity   something you do in order to avoid doing something else, which can be turned into useful time if you do things that contribute to the task at hand. Otherwise, displacement activity is purely a form of procrastination.

draft   a serious attempt to write a paper in its full form, while remaining open to possible revision.

dynamics of discussion   three principles—talk enough, don't talk too much, and stay on the topic.

early modern Europe   a period of European history running from the end of the Middle Ages (c1400) through the Renaissance, the exploration of the New World, the scientific revolution, the Enlightenment, and the French Revolution. (See also circa, Renaissance, and Enlightenment.)

endnote   a citation that explains where you got a particular idea or quotation. It is similar to a footnote, except that the citation is found at the end of the paper rather than at the bottom of the page.

essay questions   questions calling for a coherent explanation of a concept or topic, supported by details, that addresses important issues raised in the course. Instructions may include one or more of the following: compare, contrast, discuss, explain, evaluate, show, etc.

exam performance strategies   choices and behaviors implemented during the exam so that you will be as efficient, accurate, and effective as possible.

exam preparation strategies   choices and behaviors implemented before an exam to maximize success and minimize anxiety, including systematic study and good time management.

fascism   a radical political movement that combined intense nationalism with a love of violence and the persecution of minorities or rival political movements. Mussolini's Italian Fascist party first used this name, and it has been applied to a number of similar movements in the 1920s and 1930s, including Hitler's National Socialist Party in Germany.

footnote   a citation that explains where you got a particular idea or quotation. It is similar to an endnote, except that the citation is found at the bottom of the page rather than at the end of the paper

freewriting   early writing that is kept in the form of journal entries or notes and is intended for the first stages of thinking and gathering information on a topic.

gender   the roles given to men and women in a particular society. It stands in contrast to sex, which represents the biological differences between men and women.

gender-minority discussion issues   groups who have traditionally been silenced may need to cultivate conscious strategies for building confidence and participating in discussions.

historical abbreviations   shorthand form of words commonly used in or special to history classes that can facilitate efficient note taking.

humanists   thinkers or artists who focus on the potentialities of human beings rather than on God or nature. Many of the important figures of the Renaissance are called humanists to distinguish them from figures of the Middle Ages, who treated almost everything as a matter of religion. (See also Middle Ages and Renaissance.)

hypothetical questions   essay questions that ask you to use knowledge of course materials and your own reasoning powers to apply course content to novel situations. Also called *problem-solving questions.*

Industrial Revolution   a radical change in the way that goods were produced. It involved breaking up manufacturing processes into small tasks and having a worker repeat a single task over and over, rather than producing an entire object. The Industrial Revolution led to new and larger industries, a wave of inventions, and some of the greatest changes ever seen in everyday life. It began in Britain sometime in the eighteenth century and spread, first to Western Europe and North America, and then to much of the rest of the world. Some historians distinguish between a First Industrial Revolution, which involved producing existing goods more efficiently, and a

Second Industrial Revolution beginning in the late nineteenth century, which produced entirely new goods, particularly in the chemical and electrical industries.

intellectual history   the study of the ideas of earlier eras. This may concentrate on the great thinkers of a period or include the attitudes and assumptions of larger groups. (See also assumptions.)

interpretations   these are ways of explaining the evidence about a particular period. There generally is more than one interpretation of any set of events in the past. The job of the historian or the student of history is to decide which one provides the most reasonable explanation of what happened.

interpretive multiple-choice items   items that require you to interpret statements and ideas, solve problems, or apply concepts to new situations in order to select the right response.

IPSO   a tool for analyzing or presenting arguments, consisting of Issue, Position, Support, and Outcome.

key concept card   a note card that features a major concept, person, or event along with supporting details or other related information.

learned helplessness   an inability to act or solve problems stemming from low self-confidence and discouragement. It is "learned" because one has talked oneself into this state of mind. Thus, it can be unlearned.

lower middle class   a social class of small shopkeepers and low-level civil servants (some schoolteachers and minor officials). Also called *petit bourgeoisie.*

main thesis   the primary position taken in a paper or essay. This will be the guiding idea of the paper and the point to which the conclusion refers.

Middle Ages   a period of European history situated between the fall of the Roman Empire and the Renaissance and dominated by Christianity. Different historians would have different ideas about when the Middle Ages began and when they ended, but most would agree that it ran roughly from A.D. 400 to sometime between 1300 and 1500. The adjective form of this term is medieval. (See also Renaissance.)

military history   the study of past wars. In the past, this kind of history generally focused on the strategies of military leaders, but increasingly it includes such topics as civilian life at the home front, the mobilization of the population for war, and the impact of war on the average person.

motivation   a state of mind that leads to action. Related to the word *move,* motivation is the willingness to do something that is the necessary beginning of any accomplishment.

nationalism   an intense devotion to one's own country above all others, often expressed in hatred toward other peoples.

Pablo Picasso   a Spanish artist (1881–1973) who was one of the foremost figures in modern art at the beginning of the twentieth century. He was one of the founders of cubism in painting.

patricians   the ancient Roman aristocracy. (See also aristocrats and plebeians.)

peasant   small farmers who raise most of their own food and who are generally forced to share their produce with aristocrats or landowners. (See also aristocrats.)

periodical   a newspaper, magazine, or other publication that is published in a series of issues.

plagiarism   the intentional or unintentional use of others' ideas and words as your own, considered to be a serious transgression in any academic field. Don't do it!

plebeians   the nonaristocrats in ancient Rome who struggled to gain power from the aristocrats who had long ruled the city. (See also aristocrats and patricians.)

political history   the study of governments and the actions of their leaders in earlier periods in time. This may focus on the actions of major leaders, the struggles between various groups for power, or the ways in which ordinary citizens interacted with their government.

popular culture   the art, stories, and entertainment of average citizens at a particular period. It is distinguished from the elite culture, which was enjoyed only by a small number of rich or highly cultured individuals.

predrafting   the first attempt to put together a paper, not yet a draft because it is still open to considerable revision.

primary sources   original documents written during a particular period, ranging from records and legal documents to biographies and literature. (See also secondary sources.)

procrastination   putting off what needs to be done. In college, it applies especially to reading and to major projects for which there is seemingly a lot of lead time. Conquering procrastination is a major solution to time-management problems.

progress   the steady improvement of human life, often as a result of science.

proletariat   members of the industrial working class. They worked, generally for low wages, in the mines and factories produced by the Industrial Revolution. (See also Industrial Revolution.)

Puritan   a member of a Protestant group that appeared in sixteenth-century England. The Puritans believed that God had determined who would be saved and who would be damned before the beginning of time. They stressed moral purity and rejected the existing English Church as too sinful. The Puritans provided most of the first wave of immigrants to New England.

recall multiple-choice items   the simplest kind of multiple-choice question, which poses a question or gives a stem followed by a list of possible responses that call for remembering information.

Renaissance   a period of European history running roughly from the fourteenth to the sixteenth centuries that was marked by a revival of art and learning.

role-playing   participating as a particular character or from a particular perspective in a simulation of an event or period.

Scholastic   having to do with a school of medieval philosophy.

secondary sources   historical studies about a particular period. These are studied to get various interpretations of the past and to see what kinds of evidence have been used to support each. Secondary sources are based on primary sources. (See also primary sources.)

serfs   peasants who worked a small plot of land that was owned by an aristocrat. They were not slaves, since they could not be bought and sold. But they were not fully free, since they could not leave their land and had to provide the aristocrat with part of their produce and/or labor. Serfdom was common in Europe in the Middle Ages. (See also peasant, aristocrat, and Middle Ages.)

short-answer questions   various kinds of items that require you to produce information in an uncomplicated format, such as identifications and definitions.

social class   a group of individuals who share a way of earning a living. Most members of a social class generally share certain attitudes and have a similar role in the political system.

social history   the study of the history of large social groups. It may focus on the conflicts among different classes or on the conditions of everyday life. (See also social class.)

Spanish Civil War   a bloody conflict that began in 1936 when General Francisco Franco led a rebellion of conservatives against the democratically elected government in Spain. Nazi Germany and Fascist Italy sent him support, while only the Soviet Union assisted the Loyalists, who were fighting against him. The German bombing of the town of Guernica gave a frightening view of what would happen in the Second World War and became a symbol of the more than 600,000 lives lost before Franco forces won in 1939.

strategy   a conscious, thoughtful plan for approaching a task or problem, along with tactics for carrying out the plan successfully.

study group   A carefully selected and organized small group of peers who engage in collaborative learning, provide mutual support, and take equal responsibility for the work of the group.

study guide   an organized set of notes and other documents that brings together all study activities for a course, often including lecture notes, reading notes, key concept cards, sample or earlier exams, and class handouts.

subject catalog   an index to the books in a library arranged by topic. It may be found in a card catalog or in a computerized catalog system.

super map   a comprehensive visual diagram that represents the main issues and events for the material on which an exam will be given, often constructed from more specific maps made during study.

syllabus   the schedule of readings, assignments, and tests that an instructor provides with a course.

Taoist   a school of traditional Chinese philosophy that stressed harmony with nature and a simple life. It provided an alternative to Confucianism, which concentrated on social rules. (See also Confucianism.)

three levels of planning   in college, you will need to plan on a semester basis (the master-plan), on a weekly basis (establishing your routine), and on a daily basis (putting into order of priority what must be done each day).

time management   combining concentration and organization in a way that enables you to make maximum use of time for getting the important things done.

utopian community   a group of people who have left society in order to create a perfect society based on a set of principles. Many utopian communities were formed in the nineteenth century around religious or socialist beliefs.

Western civilization   a course that traces the history of European peoples and the earlier cultures from which they developed. Such courses usually begin with the ancient New East and then study the history of ancient Greece and Rome, medieval, early modern, and modern Europe.

world civilization   a course that traces the development of the entire human species from its origins to the present.

World War I   a terribly destructive war that involved almost all of Europe, many European colonies, and the United States. It lasted from 1914 to 1918, and its effects continued to destabilize European political systems and society for a quarter of a century after peace was declared.

INDEX

Abbreviations, 117–118
Active listening, 115–116
African-American history, 27
Analogy in historical events,
    165–166
Analytical reading, 87–93
Annotating, 93–96
Anxiety and exam taking, 140
Art, making use of in a history
    course, 21–24, 66

Biorhythm patterns, 49

Classes, social, 25–26, 28
Collaborative note taking, 119
Concentration, 53
Cultural history, 17–25
Current events and history, 165

Dates, 6–8
Diplomatic history, 17–19
Discussion, gender-minority
    issues, 130–132
Discussion and note taking,
    132–133
Discussion dynamics, 127–129
Discussion benefits, 124–126
Discussion preparation, 126–127
Discussion and role playing,
    133–134
Displacement activity, 51–52

Emotions and academic success,
    41–43

Endnotes, 186–190
Energy, 40–41
Essay questions, 155–166
    Nine basic instructions,
        156–158
    Hypothetical questions,
        163–165
    Organizing answers, 161
    Outlining answers, 161–163
Exam review strategies,
    146–147
Exam questions, 148–166
Exam performance strategies,
    145–147
Exam preparation strategies,
    140–145

Family history, 27
Footnotes, 186–190

Gaining mastery, 43
Gender, 29–30
Geography, 5–6
Goals, goal setting, 38–39

History, changing nature of,
    14–17

Intellectual history, 17–25
IPSO, 89, 115

Key concept cards, 96–98

Learned helplessness, 37–38

Listen first, read later strategy, 109–110
Long-term exam strategies, 142–144

Mapping techniques, 99–105
Memorization, 18–19
Military history, 17–19
Motivation, 36–38
Multiple choice questions, 148–152
  Recall, 148
  Interpretive, 148–152

Notes in margin of textbooks, 65

Open-book exams, 167–168

Paper writing, basic components of, 172–176
  Finding a topic, 177–180
  First draft, 183–184
  Preparation for writing, 180–183
  Rewriting, 184–186
Plagiarism, 186–189
Political history, 17–19
Popular culture, 24–25
Primary sources, 106–108
Priority setting, 50
Procrastination, 50

Rational self-talk, 42
Read first, listen later strategy, 108–109

Read-listen-read strategy, 110–111
Recognition and recall exam questions, 148
Reporter's techniques, 115–117
Research, 190–194
Reviewing notes, 118

Scheduling, 44–48
  Weekly, 45–47
  Daily, 46–47
Secondary sources, 106–108
Short-answer questions, 154–155
Short-term exam strategies, 142
Sleep study, 41
Social history, 25–28
Strategic reading, 86–87
Study group strategies, 134–136
  Formation, 134–135
  Membership, 135
  Structure, 135–136
  Tasks, 136
Study guide, 143–145
Syllabus, making use of, 3–4, 8–10, 30

Table of contents, making use of, 4
Take-home exams, 166–167
Time management, 44–50
True-false questions, 153–154

Underlining, 65

Women's history, 28–30